Roses

KEW GARDENING GUIDES

Roses

David Welch

Series editor John Simmons
OBE, VMH

TIMBER PRESS
Portland, Oregon

Front cover photograph: Photos Horticultural
Back cover photograph: The Harry Smith Horticultural
Photographic Collection

First published in 1988 by Collingridge Books,
Collingridge is an imprint of Octopus Illustrated Publishing
Michelin House, 81 Fulham Road, London SW3 6RB, England
part of Reed International Books,
in association with the Royal Botanic Gardens, Kew

First published in North America in 1992 by
Timber Press, Inc.
9999 S.W. Wilshire, Suite 124
Portland, Oregon 97225, USA.

ISBN 0-88192-219-6

Filmset in England by Vision Typesetting, Manchester
in 11 on 12 pt Bembo

Produced by Mandarin Offset
Printed in Hong Kong

Contents

Preface

The Royal Botanic Gardens, Kew with their herbarium, library, laboratories and unrivalled collection of living plants, form one of the world's most important centres of botanical science. Their origins, however, can be traced back to a modest nine-acre site in the Pleasure Garden at Kew which Augusta, the Dowager Princess of Wales and mother of King George III, set aside for the cultivation of new and interesting plants.

On this site were grown many of the exotic species which reached England for the first time during this period of mercantile and colonial expansion. Trees such as our oldest specimens of *Sophora japonica* from China and *Robinia pseudoacacia* from America were planted for the Princess and still flourish at Kew, as do many accessions from Africa and Australia.

Many of Kew's earliest collectors were botanical explorers who made difficult and dangerous journeys to remote and unknown parts of the world in their search for economically important or beautiful plants. The work of Kew's botanists in gathering new species was complemented by that of Kew's gardeners, who were responsible for their care and propagation. The gardeners were also responsible for trans-shipping living plants from Kew to other parts of the world, and the Gardens rapidly became a clearing house through which 'useful' species grown in one continent were transferred to another.

At the present time, the living collections of the Royal Botanic Gardens contain approximately 50,000 types of flowering plants from every corner of the earth. Such a collection makes unending demands on the skills and dedication of those entrusted with its care. It also provides an unrivalled opportunity for gardening staff to familiarize themselves with the diverse requirements of plants from the many different climatic and geological regions of the world. The plants in the Royal Botanic Gardens are no museum collection, however. As in the eighteenth and nineteenth centuries, the Gardens continue to distribute living plant material on a worldwide basis, though they now use modern facilities such as the micropropagation unit at Kew and the Seed Bank at Wakehurst Place. The Gardens are also actively involved in the conservation of the world's plant resources and in supplying scientists at Kew and elsewhere with the plants and plant material required for their research. This may range from basic studies of the ways in which plants have evolved to the isolation of plant chemicals of potential use in agriculture and medicine. Whatever the purpose of the research, there is inevitably a need to grow plants and to grow them well, whether they be plants from the rain forests of the Amazon or from the deserts of Africa.

Your interest in gardening may be neither scientific nor economic, but I believe that the expert advice provided by specialist authors in this new series of *Kew Gardening Guides* will provide help of a quality that can be given only by gardeners with long experience of the art and science of cultivating a particular group of plants.

E. Arthur Bell
Director, Royal Botanic Gardens, Kew

Opposite: The early flowering *Rosa hugonis* from the *Botanical Magazine* (Plate 7241)

Foreword

Gardening is in part instinctive, in part experience. Look in any village or town and you will see many gardens, balconies or even windowsills full of healthy plants brightening up the streets. However, there are always likely to be other plots that are sterile and devoid of plants, or overgrown and unloved. Admittedly gardening is laborious, but the hours spent sweating behind a mower on a hot summer's day will be amply rewarded when the smooth green lawn is admired; the painful nettle stings incurred while clearing ground will soon be forgotten when the buds of newly planted shrubs burst forth in spring.

These few examples of the joy and pain of gardening are all part of its attraction to its devotees. The successful gardeners and plant lovers of this world come to understand plants instinctively, learning their likes and dislikes, their lifespan and ultimate size, recognizing and correcting ailments before they become serious. They work with the seasons of the year, not against them; they think ahead, driven by caring, being aware of when conditions are right for planting, mowing or harvesting and, perhaps most important of all, they know when to leave well alone.

This understanding of the natural order cannot be learned overnight. It is a continuous two-way process that lasts a lifetime. In creating a garden, past masters such as Humphry Repton in the eighteenth century or Gertrude Jekyll in the nineteenth perceived and enhanced the natural advantages of a site, and Jekyll in particular was an acute observer of the countryside and its seasons. Seeing a plant in its natural situation gives knowledge of its needs in cultivation. And then, once design and planting have formed a garden, the process reverses as the garden becomes the inspiration for learning about the natural world.

With the widespread loss of the world's natural habitats now causing the daily extinction of species, botanic gardens and other specialist gardens are becoming as arks, holding irreplaceable collections. Thus gardens are increasingly cooperating to form networks which can retain as great a diversity of plants as possible. More than ever gardens can offer a refuge for our beleaguered flora and fauna and, whether a garden be great or small, formal or natural, this need should underpin its enduring qualities of peace and harmony – the challenge of the creative unison of formal and natural areas.

The authors of these volumes have all become acknowledged specialists in particular aspects of gardening and their texts draw on their experience and impart the vitality that sustains their own enthusiasm and dedication. It is hoped, therefore, that these *Kew Gardening Guides* will be the means of sharing their hard-earned knowledge and understanding with a wider audience.

Like a many faceted gemstone, horticulture has many sides, each with its own devotees, but plants are the common link, and they define this series of horticultural books and the work of Kew itself.

John Simmons
Editor

Introduction

The Empress Josephine would hardly recognize the plants in the modern rose garden. Apart from lending her name to the most enduring catch-phrase of this century, in the last she pioneered the idea of growing roses in a garden specially made to show off their qualities. She planted it with as many sorts as she could gather, and her patronage provided the thrust that projected them to the top of the floral popularity league. The kind of roses that she grew were given their own immortality by the French artist Redouté in *Les Roses* (1817–24). His famous illustrations captured the state of the genus at that time, and provided a yardstick against which the changes brought about by modern rose breeders can be measured.

Josephine would find few, if any, of the varieties she cultivated listed in modern catalogues, with the exception of those that specialize in old-fashioned roses. She would find the colour range expanded into vermilion and cerise and lurid shades of orange, and the flower shape transformed. She would be astonished to find modern hybrids in flower more or less continuously from early summer to late autumn. Pygmy roses were introduced, probably from China, in her time, but she would not recognize the miniatures as they exist today, nor know what was meant by ground cover, patio or cluster flowered hybrids.

Recent progress in genetic engineering suggests that the pace of change will even accelerate. It is possible that the blue rose sought by generations of gardeners will make its appearance once molecular scientists direct their attention to the problem and introduce the missing pigment delphinidin into the genus. Even longer periods of flowering, more vivid colours, more powerful scents and better foliage can all be envisaged for the future.

Roses have a universal popularity. Their colour range is wide, they are adaptable, they vary in habit between miniatures suitable for a trough or sink garden to mammoths that will engulf a tree. They suit many climates and they will grow successfully on a variety of soils; they are readily available and are comparatively cheap to buy; they flower for a long season and in some cases are heavily perfumed. They are horticultural paragons. It is hardly surprising that they are popular in so many countries round the world.

1

The Story of Roses

The rose is a well-connected plant, and it has given its name to a large family that includes the apple, pear, plum, peach, cherry and strawberry as well as a number of other important fruits. It also embraces a range of hardy deciduous shrubs and trees, many of which find a place in gardens. Pre-eminent among them, however, is the rose itself. It forms a large, wide-ranging genus, though in nature its species are confined almost exclusively to the Northern Hemisphere – Europe, northern Asia including China, and North America.

There are perhaps as many as three thousand different species, though few of them are decorative enough for use in gardens. Among those that are, several have been cultivated and esteemed for thousands of years; there are references to them in ancient literature and illustrations of them on frescoes and in tombs. *Rosa gallica* is alleged to have been grown by the Medes and Persians, and if so must qualify as one of the longest cultivated of all ornamental plants. The Chinese have also grown roses for thousands of years; the first of the Eastern kinds to be introduced into Europe were obtained not as the result of a plant-hunting expedition but by purchase from oriental nurseries.

A shrub that is distributed so widely and has been cultivated for so long has, not surprisingly, acquired a considerable literature. Few ornamental plants command such an extensive bibliography, which in the case of the rose extends over two or three millennia.

In Western civilizations, the Ancient Greeks and the Romans both esteemed the rose, extolling its beauty, sometimes using it as a symbol, and proffering it to their gods. The Romans had a particularly strong line in dedication, and the symbolic use of the flower that they established has persisted to this day. It was offered to Venus as an emblem of beauty and to Cupid as a token of love; the record sales of today's red roses on St Valentine's Day echo the Roman tradition. It was dedicated to Aurora, goddess of the dawn, for in places with hot climates flowers are at their freshest and loveliest in the morning, and to Harpocrates, the god of silence. His rose suspended over a room meant that what took place below was confidential – the term *sub rosa* is still sometimes used to indicate that discussions taking place are private ones. The Romans used rose petals to shower guests at banquets; as recently as 1987 I was asked to recommend a source of them to be scattered over a bride and groom after their wedding.

Roses were the symbols used by the factions in the English Wars of the Roses – red for the House of Lancaster and white for the House of York. The colours were combined to form the unifying badge of the Tudor dynasty. In our own times, it has recently become the national flower of the United States of America, and in the 1987 British general election was worn on the lapels of many aspirants to office, though not all of them had discovered the buttonhole reservoir, a tube filled with water and pinned out of sight behind the lapel, where it can discreetly accommodate and sustain the stem of the flower.

Naturally the ancients gave hints on how to cultivate the plants, and their

Opposite: *Rosa villosa (R. pomifera)* from the *Botanical Magazine* (Plate 8004)

15

Enclosed garden with roses. A 16th century woodcut from *Le Roman de la Rose*

advice has an echo today. Theophrastus, for example, recommended burning the bushes to get rid of the tangled stems. Anyone who has observed the crackling intensity of a bonfire of rose prunings will know that this is a feasible proposition, especially in a hot, dry climate, and I can testify that the plants are quite likely to have recovered. As a garden boy I lit a bonfire one winter's day too close to a bush of 'Stanwell Perpetual', which caught fire as well. It made a sparkling show; the head gardener was badly stretched to find words to express his appreciation. The bush was cut down to remove the offence of blackened stems, but in spring growth started again from ground level. After a couple of years the plant was as good as new, though my relationship with the head gardener never recovered.

Today's parallel is the draconian method of pruning recommended by a famous French firm for what it calls landscaping roses. If they grow bigger than required the stems can simply be mown away, using flail mowers like those used by road authorities to give an annual cut to grass verges, which reduce the vegetation to fragments. They do the same for roses, but the bushes send up new shoots from their stumps and from below ground level.

Although the rose has such an ancient association with man, it was not until the beginning of the 19th century that the modern explosion of cultivars was made possible, when the hardy roses of Europe with their short flowering season were brought into contact with the long-flowering, rather tender species from China. It was an essential step because few of the wild roses of Europe justify inclusion in gardens: their flowers are beautiful but fleeting, their fruits pretty but unspectacular. Even today only one of them is widely cultivated, and then not for decoration. It is the dog rose, *R. canina*, which together with its selected forms 'Pollmeriana', 'Schmids Ideal', 'Brogs', 'Pfänders' and others is one of the principal rootstocks used in propagating roses by budding. It is a tough customer, and is popular because its roots are death-defiant and have impressive powers of regeneration even when they have been knocked about during transplanting. In the old days it was one of the common plants of Europe, growing on the fringe of woodland, scrambling through and over the scrub, from which rosehips, long known for their medicinal properties, were gathered.

Modern agricultural practices – ripping out hedges, using selective weedkillers, turning scrubland into farmland – have robbed roses of their natural habitats in many parts of the world. The spectacular advance of garden roses this century has been matched by a sad retreat in the wild.

2
Roses in the Garden

Roses can be used in a variety of ways. They are by no means confined to rosebeds, even though this is the most usual place for many of them. They also have a range of attributes, such as fragrance or their ability to fill an awkward space, that make them attractive to gardeners.

ROSEBEDS

The conventional way of using rose bushes is in beds. There they are planted for bold displays, and breeders have provided cultivars that rival the geranium in the extent and intensity of their colour range. If the garden is big enough they are best planted in beds that contain only a single cultivar, but where limited space makes this impractical and a mixture has to be used care is needed to match them for height and compatibility of colour. Beds that are not more than 2 m (6 ft) wide permit cultivation to be carried out from either side without the need to move among the plants. Larger-scale planting is possible, but in this case the use of weedkillers is advisable to reduce summer cultivation to a minimum. Generally speaking, the smaller the size of the garden the smaller the beds should be, and shorter cultivars of roses should also be used. It is all a matter of proportion.

CONTAINERS

Roses can be grown in containers, and the miniatures are particularly well adapted for the purpose. Troughs, sinks, tubs, terracotta pots, window boxes and a variety of other items can be used. Bigger roses can also be grown in this way, but they are not the best plants to choose if all-year-round interest is required. For gardeners who wish to obtain extra early cut flowers, roses can also be grown in pots and put into a greenhouse for gentle forcing in late winter.

All containers should be well drained by means of holes placed in the bottom or at the sides near the base. If these are not present they should be made. Although the use of coarse, rough material at the bottom of the container to help drainage is now no longer regarded as essential, it is worth using where the plant is to be a permanent resident. Coarse peat, pieces of rotted turf, even gravel, can be used for the purpose.

The container should be filled with rich compost. My first experience of gardening was breaking up pieces of dried, well-rotted dung, which then formed a third by bulk of a compost intended for roses. At the time it made me wonder if I had entered the right trade, but the roses later flourished. If the container is a deep one, well-rotted manure can be used at the base, and although the idea seems old fashioned it works well. Any good potting compost will provide the rest.

If the plant is already in a container it can be repotted at any time; otherwise,

Opposite: Part of The Royal National Rose Society's collection of roses at St Albans, Hertfordshire

planting is best done in the spring just before growth starts. The compost should be moist but not saturated. The classic test is to squeeze a handful of it. If it retains the shape of the hand it is moist enough. If it then fails to shatter into fragments when it is dropped, it is too wet and should be dried a little before use. Immediately after planting, the container should be watered thoroughly from above so that the compost is further settled around the roots.

Subsequent watering often causes trouble. Roses use a lot of water when they are growing rapidly in the spring and need daily attention, but later, as growth ripens, they use less. In winter, when they are dormant, they hardly use any at all, though the compost should not be allowed to dry out for fear of desiccating the roots.

To get flowers early in the year a greenhouse is necessary, though it is possible to use a bright windowsill for the purpose. The plants should be grown in pots 25 cm (10 in) or 30 cm (1 ft) across. During the summer they are plunged into the earth out of doors to reduce the amount of watering that is needed and also to keep them securely upright. In late winter they are brought indoors. If a warm greenhouse is available, growth is quick. Temperatures can be gradually increased to about 18°C (65°F), but should not be higher or very soft, weak stems will develop. On sunny days plenty of ventilation is needed, and spreading water on the paths in the middle of the day helps to keep the greenhouse cooler and produces a buoyant atmosphere much esteemed by both gardeners and roses. In a cold greenhouse the practice is the same, though roses respond more slowly. Either way they will flower earlier than is possible out of doors, and the flowers are more nearly perfect because they are not subject to damage by the weather. Once they do flower, every effort should be made to keep the greenhouse as cool as possible so that the flowers keep their freshness longer.

GROUND COVER

In the last decade or so a new concept has been addressed to gardeners. It is the idea of ground-cover roses, which is worth considering when planting a bank or filling up an odd corner or when a mass of colour is needed. The best cultivars reduce maintenance by smothering the ground, and because they are usually grown on their own roots suckers are not a problem. They vary in height depending on the cultivar, but the bigger kinds form several layers of arching, spreading stems that can suppress the growth of annual weeds – 'Swany', for example, can be 2 m (6 ft) across and 60 cm (2 ft) high.

Few of these roses provide a sufficiently dense cover to prevent strong perennial weeds from growing, so it is necessary to remove all the roots and underground stems of such weeds as docks, thistles and bindweed before planting the roses. Couch grass can also be a nuisance; if it is, the weedkiller called dalapon will kill it effectively. I recommend its use because of the great difficulty of ensuring that every bit of the grass is removed, and because any pieces that are left behind will grow and spread rapidly and be difficult to deal with once entangled in the roses. Planting the roses is done in the normal way.

There are many cultivars that can be used as ground cover, though some of them can become as high as 1.2 m (4 ft) and are by no means dwarf. Suitable varieties include 'Bonica', 'Ferdy', 'Fiona', 'Nozomi', 'Red Blanket', 'Swany' and a number of others. The range is being increased year by year as breeders develop the possibilities of the type – and of course are attracted by high potential sales.

Apart from minor work to remove dead wood, these roses do not need regular pruning. Indeed, that would defeat the object of smothering the ground with stems and leaves. The best cultivars are wreathed in flowers over a long season.

Ground fillers

I used to have a cat called George. My neighbour, who also thought that he owned it, called it Gus. Of course no one really owns anything of such an independent mind as a cat. This one spent just enough time with each of us to give the impression that it belonged to both. *Rosa rugosa* is like George. It is an instinctive stray. It forms an expanding thicket of spiny stems carrying dark green leaves, large, bright, tousled flowers and very large hips. Its forms and hybrids are numerous and all have the same characteristics.

In bigger gardens a space occasionally exists that needs to be filled cheaply with something that will look after itself and provide interest without needing attention. One or two roses have the necessary attributes and should be considered for such locations. *Rosa rugosa* and its progeny are the principal candidates, and have the added bonus of a significant scent when a large number are planted together. *R. pimpinellifolia* and its offspring will also do the job, though with less enthusiasm. They are lower in stature and so are less useful as a background for other plants.

Some of the ground-cover roses can also be used where height is not important, but care should be taken to choose those that are vigorous enough to fend for themselves. Some of them are not good at keeping weeds down because their cover is rather thin and low and weeds can push through it and flourish. Nothing looks worse. For corner filling choose 'Bonica', 'Ferdy', 'Fiona', 'Red Blanket', 'Rosy Cushion' or 'Smarty'.

Hedges

Many kinds of rose can be used to make informal hedges. The best are those that are naturally bushy and do not need annual pruning. Clipping is possible in the case of shrub roses, but it robs the plant of its natural grace and may also cut away a crop of flowers and hips. For use on boundaries taller cultivars can be used, and there are many prickly kinds that will repel intruders. Because they are deciduous in many climates, they are not suitable where an all-year-round screen is needed to give privacy or to block a view. For this purpose evergreen plants should be chosen instead. Roses can also be used to provide divisions within a garden, in which case the cultivar should be selected to fit the scale of the space available.

Making a hedge requires the same soil preparation and planting techniques as for general work. The difference is that the plants are put in a line. Cultivation should encompass a strip a metre wide and as long as the hedge is to be. The plants can be put in a double row, the spacings staggered to produce a thicker, rather dense hedge such as may be required on a boundary. A single line, which consumes less space, is best for use within the garden. Close planting is required to ensure that the hedge is a thing of substance and is not thin or gappy. For a single line of smaller-growing species or bush roses a gap of 45 cm (18 in) between plants is sufficient. Double rows should be 30 cm (1 ft) apart, with the plants within them 60 cm (2 ft) apart. Large-growing shrub roses should be 1 m (3 ft) apart.

All the modern cultivars are suitable, especially the vigorous ones such as 'Alexander', 'Golden Jubilee', 'Queen Elizabeth' and 'Southampton'. All shrub roses can also be used. For small hedges *Rosa nitida*, which grows to 60 cm (2 ft) high, makes an attractive – though not a very showy – contribution to a garden. It is one of the species introduced from North America, and like many of its compatriots the foliage develops strong autumn colours. The hybrids of *R. pimpinellifolia* (*R. spinosissima*) are taller and make useful hedges because of their crowded prickles. They will also grow on sandy soils. The biggest is little more than 1.5 m (5 ft) tall. Two others at the same height are *R. glauca* (*R. rubrifolia*), which has silvery purple leaves that make an interesting foil for other plants, and the forms and hybrids of *R. rugosa*, which form spiny thickets for use on a boundary. Taller hedges can be provided by *R. xanthina* forma *spontanea* 'Canary Bird'. Its graceful arching stems can reach 2.5 m (8 ft) high, as can those of *R. eglanteria*, the sweet briar, which makes a dense, intruder-resistant boundary.

A delightful cottage garden display with 'Masquerade' (see page 96) as its centrepiece

An archway
wreathed in roses

PERGOLAS

Pergolas should really lead to something important enough to justify the emphasis they give. The more vigorous climbing roses can be trained up and over them. The structure should, of course, be strong enough to sustain the weight it will have to carry, and should be built of materials that do not require regular maintenance – stone or brick pillars with oak beams between them. Cheaper wood is ultimately more expensive because of the maintenance it needs. When choosing the dimensions of a pergola it is important to remember that the foliage and stems of the climbers will hang down, and room should be left to accommodate both them and passers by.

Climbing roses can also be grown against poles, erected either singly or as tripods, though attaching the stems can be an awkward and disagreeable job. They help to give extra height to a planting scheme and can be used as points of emphasis, like horticultural exclamation marks. Wooden posts with swags of strong rope between them can also be used.

RAMBLERS ON TREES

First choose your tree. It must be sound and strong, because the rose is an extra burden on the branches and the increase in wind resistance exerts pressure on the roots. *Rosa filipes* 'Kiftsgate' and *R.* 'Wedding Day' are capable of scrambling high into the brances of a tree – and of covering a garden shed, for that matter.

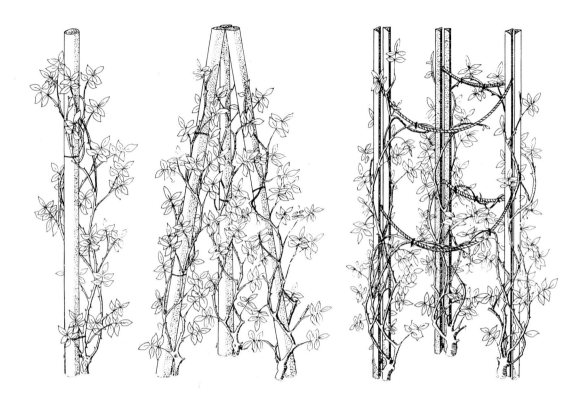

Roses can be trained up a single pillar, a tripod or to hang from swags of strong rope

For smaller trees, shrubs and hedges, less vigorous roses should be used, such as 'New Dawn'.

The rose should be planted away from the trunk in a position where it can get moisture. The ground should be well prepared, and plenty of organic matter should be used to increase the amount of water held by the soil where the roots can get it easily. The stems are trained towards the tree as they develop on canes or stakes. Growth will be slow at first, but speeds up as the plant establishes itself. Once they reach the branch system, the roses will sprawl and scramble through the tree without any need to tie them in place.

Replacing grass

Lawns are time-consuming to maintain because of the regular attention they need. Roses can be used to replace grass in places where mowing is difficult: ground-cover roses can be used on banks, as long as they are not too steep and dry, and bush or shrub roses can be used to round off corners or to fill areas that are awkward in shape. I even plant them in the centre reservation of dual carriageways, where they are very much cheaper to keep than grass would be. They are more expensive to provide and plant, of course, but after about four years they go into credit, the extra initial costs having been recovered.

Roses on walls

Roses, like other climbing plants, can be used to soften the outline of a building and to clothe a wall. Many modern climbers are free flowering, and though the name 'ever-blooming' given to them in some catalogues is an exaggeration they certainly have a long season in flower. Against a background of brick or stone they can make a rich, brilliant show. They should preferably face east or west, where they get enough sunshine without being roasted as they might be on a wall that faces south, though in higher latitudes a south wall does very well. North walls are difficult for most cultivars; for this aspect other plants should be chosen.

Roses will not cling by themselves, though they will scramble over other bushes and trees. If grown against a wall or pillar they need to be fastened into place, but because the stems are firm and woody the ties do not need to be numerous. Support has to be given by means of wires stretched horizontally and held in place by pins called vine eyes, which are hammered into the mortar joints at intervals of 1 m (3 ft) or so. The pin has a hole at the end through which the wire is threaded. The best kind to use is plastic-coated wire, preferably a black colour, which merges with most unpainted backgrounds. It is possible to obtain green, but this looks ill at ease in a garden because its lurid shade is unlike anything in nature. The wire should be made as taut as possible, and straining bolts can be used provided that a firm anchorage is created for them. This may be rather hard to do when fixing the wires on an existing wall, in which case a pair of pliers should be used to pull the wire as tight as it will go and then to twist the end round itself to fix it to the pin. The wires should be spaced at vertical intervals of about 45 cm (18 in).

The roses can be tied to the wires with a variety of materials. For example, there are specially made twists with a central core of wire for tying any plant to a support. Tarred twine is much cheaper, and though it is more trouble to use it is very durable. All the necessary materials can be obtained at an ironmonger.

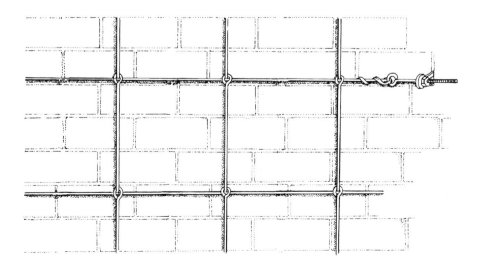

Roses need support to cover a wall. Wires stretched between vine eyes will do the job admirably

Climbing rose
'New Dawn' (see
page 97)

An alternative way of supporting the roses is to attach them to a trellis fixed to the face of the wall. Roses can also be trained against fences, especially the popular close-boarded kinds, which are much improved by being concealed.

SEASIDE PLANTING

I used to work at the seaside resort of Blackpool in Lancashire. The town faces westwards, and every month or so the sea, tormented by gales, flings itself against the sea wall, throwing spume high into the air. This is gathered by the wind and swept across the town. It is exhilarating for the residents, but few plants can survive unless they have shelter.

Rosa rugosa is among a handful of plants that can withstand wind and salt and act as a front line of defence. In such extreme conditions the rose does not attain its full beauty or even its potential height. Sometimes it is cut down to ground level, but it normally revives and patiently grows again, restoring its energy and courage in good seasons to face the bad ones. In seaside places shelter is all-important in order to give vulnerable plants enough protection to grow. *Rosa rugosa* filters the wind, slows it down, traps the salt spray, and allows other plants to flourish in its lee.

Rosa pimpinellifolia, also known as the burnet rose, grows naturally on rather sandy soil near the sea, and is another good plant to use in the front rank of a screen intended to give shelter.

SPECIMEN PLANTING

Roses grown in small clumps can make an attractive feature in a lawn or among smaller plants. They should be put in close so that they unite and appear at a casual glance to be a single large shrub. The best effect is obtained with cultivars with graceful stems that are interesting throughout the year, even during seasons when there is no flower or fruit. 'Frühlingsgold' is one of the best. It can easily exceed 2 m (7 ft) in height, however, and grows quickly, so it requires a big space and will dominate and clutter a small garden. 'Canary Bird' has the necessary grace but is also tall. For a smaller garden 'Ferdy', which can grow to 1.5 m (5 ft), has arching branches that are wreathed along their whole length with double pink flowers. For still smaller spaces 'Cécile Brunner' grows to only 1 m (3 ft). This cultivar is over a hundred years old, but its tiny pink flowers have kept it in catalogues. Growing it in a clump permits the flower to be seen and admired close at hand.

Many other roses can be treated in the same way, but the method makes them prominent and care should be taken to choose a cultivar that is capable of providing interest over a long period, with attractive foliage in the spring, a long season of flowering, and bright hips in the autumn.

The fragrant shrub rose 'Frühlingsgold' (see page 116)

FRAGRANCE

The most frequent complaint I hear about roses is that modern cultivars have no scent. This is of course not true, and many recent ones are strongly perfumed. 'Alec's Red' is a good example. Everyone has a different appreciation of fragrance, and weather conditions can affect the degree and intensity of the perfume and the extent to which it lingers, so that comparisons between cultivars are rather difficult to make. It is probable that dressings of potash, which encourage flower production and help the wood to ripen, also enrich the perfume of the flowers.

The following are some of the cultivars that I find particularly fragrant and would concentrate together to make a scented garden. I have confined the list to those that can easily be obtained from nurseries.

Climbers
'Compassion', 'Étoile de Hollande', *R. filipes* 'Kiftsgate', 'Guinée', 'Madame Grégoire Staechelin', 'New Dawn', 'Wedding Day', 'Zéphirine Drouhin'.

Bush roses
'Amber Queen', 'Alec's Red', 'Ballerina', 'Blue Moon', 'Dutch Gold', 'Fragrant Cloud', 'Fragrant Delight', 'Harry Edland', 'Korresia', 'Margaret Merril', 'Mountbatten', 'Paul Shirville', 'Radox Bouquet', 'Rebecca Claire', 'Red Devil', 'Regensberg', 'Rosemary Harkness', 'Royal William', 'Sheila's Perfume', 'Super Star', 'Sutter's Gold', 'Sweetheart', 'Wendy Cussons'.

Shrub roses
'Belle de Crécy', 'Blanche Moreau', 'Boule de Neige', 'Cardinal de Richelieu', *R. centifolia*, 'Constance Spry', 'Felicia', 'Frühlingsgold', 'Frühlingsmorgen', 'Golden Wings', 'Graham Thomas', 'Koenigin von Danemarck', 'Lady Hillingdon', 'Lady Penzance', 'Penelope', *R. primula*, 'Prosperity', 'Madame Abel Chatenay', 'Souvenir de la Malmaison', 'Stanwell Perpetual', *R. rugosa* hybrids – 'Blanc Double de Coubert', 'Fru Dagmar Hastrup', 'Roseraie de L'Haÿ', 'Scabrosa'.

Scented foliage
Rosa eglanteria (*R. rubiginosa*) has strongly scented foliage, a characteristic that is shared by its hybrids. 'Lady Penzance' and 'Meg Merrilies' are particularly recommended. The leaves of *R. primula* also have a strong scent.

HIPS

Because of their hips, some roses are as bright in the autumn as they are when in flower, and in the case of *R. rubrifolia* even better. *R. moyesii* and its progeny 'Geranium', 'Sealing Wax', 'Highdownensis' and forma *rosea* (*R. holodonta*) are probably the best, with large, red, bottle-shaped hips. The forms of *R. rugosa* have large, showy hips as well, the best being 'Frau Dagmar Hastrup' and 'Scabrosa'. Other good ones are *R. eglanteria*, *R. filipes* and its cultivars, 'Madame Grégoire Staechelin', *R. helenae*, *R. nitida*, 'Penelope', *R. pimpinellifolia*, *R. villosa* (*R. pomifera*), *R. glauca* (*R. rubrifolia*), 'Scarlet Fire' ('Scharlachglut').

Spring foliage

As roses are in flower for only part of the year the spring foliage is important, extending the period of garden interest by several weeks. It is more variable in quality and colour than most of us give it credit for. *Rosa × alba*, which is a shrub rose, has grey-green leaves; *Rosa glauca* (*R. rubrifolia*) has a purple tinge. Many bush roses have quite strongly coloured young leaves. For example, the young foliage of 'Silver Jubilee', 'Super Star', 'Glenfiddich', 'Elizabeth of Glamis' and many others are shades of bronze or copper, and the fresh green of 'Honeymoon' and others offers a pleasant contrast to them.

The dainty leaves of *Rosa moyesii* and its hybrids and of *R. elegantula* 'Persetosa' (*R. farreri* forma *persetosa*), or the deeply veined leaves of the *R. rugosa* hybrids, help to give textural contrast in a shrub border.

Autumn colour

Not many roses have bright autumn leaves, and most turn a drab shade of decayed yellow, but one or two exceptions do stand out even though they are not worth growing for this quality alone. *R. rugosa* foliage turns bright yellow. The leaves of *R. nitida* and *R. virginiana*, the latter being the best of the two, turn red and gold in the autumn like many of their deciduous compatriots from North America.

Rose companions

Many other plants can be grown with roses to extend the period of interest or to give a change of form, texture or colour, though most bush roses look best when on their own, especially those with a rather stiff, upright habit. Shrub roses can be used in a general border very easily, and those with bright hips give a touch of colour in the autumn and early winter that is often very welcome.

Bulbous plants can be used successfully with roses, though their foliage may look rather untidy as it dies down and they can get in the way of spring cultivation. Even so, some of the varieties of snowdrop, early crocus (like *Crocus tommasinianus*), the winter aconite (*Eranthis hyemalis*), and *Cyclamen coum* and its relatives, some of which have pretty leaves, all help to extend the period of interest into a season when the roses themselves are dull.

A clump or two of *Tulipa fosteriana* 'Red Emperor', which parades in vivid scarlet in spring, could be tried. This cultivar will naturalize, and can be left to grow from year to year. Violas used to be the regular associates of roses, but they get in the way of cultivation. Lavender as an edging is better. Its grey leaves give winter interest and its flowers combine well with those of most rose cultivars.

3
The Development of Modern Roses

The rose is in a constant state of change, and many new cultivars are introduced every year. This is partly because breeders look for genuine advances in quality, partly because there is a constant search for novelty, and fashions change in roses as in other things, and partly because a good new cultivar can bring commercial advantage for the breeder through royalties. Not many roses stay the course. A few do and become famous – 'Peace', 'Superstar' and 'Queen Elizabeth' are examples – but most are quite quickly superseded, so a descriptive list written today can become out of date in a few short years. In order to allow customers to trace roses and to find someone who still grows them, the Rose Growers' Association has published a pamphlet called *Find That Rose: A Guide to Who Grows What*. It can be obtained from 303 Mile End Road, Colchester, Essex, CO4 5EA, England.

The species do not change but comparatively few can command a place in gardens because their offspring and derivatives usually outclass them, and indeed were bred and selected to do so. Even among the so-called old-fashioned roses there are some that should only be bought for the largest collections, in which comprehensiveness rather than garden decoration may be the overriding criterion. Of those that have stood the test of time, some have daintiness, like 'Cécile Brunner'; delicacy of colour, like 'Stanwell Perpetual'; brightness, like *R. moyesii*; fragrance, like 'Belle de Crécy; history, like *R. gallica*; early flowers, like *R. hugonis*; rumbustiousness, like *R. rugosa*; utility, like *R. eglanteria*; dainty, fleeting loveliness, like the flowers of *R. elegantula* 'Persetosa'; individuality, like *R. sericea* var. *omeiensis* forma *pteracantha*; or, like 'Souvenir de la Malmaison', have a story attached to them with which the gardener can beguile his visitors. Breeders have now turned their attention to shrub roses, and as a result there are new cultivars, for example 'Ingrid Bergman' and 'Bonica', with which the older roses have to compete for a garden place, whatever nostalgia may suggest.

Intrepid plant hunters have perhaps played less part in rose development than in any other extensive genus. Some species have been cultivated for centuries, but the modern range of cultivars is uniquely the product of deliberate hybridization. Even so, William Kerr sent back the double white form of *R. banksiae* when he was in China, collecting for the Royal Botanic Gardens, Kew, though the rose was already in cultivation in Canton when he came across it. Ernest Wilson introduced *R. moyesii*, *R. davidii*, *R. multibracteata* and *R. filipes*, among others. Reginald Farrer sent home *R. elegantula*, and Robert Fortune also found roses in Chinese gardens, but in the grand sweep of the genus their contributions have been slight. Its heroes are the plant breeders whose skills have made it one of the most widely grown of all ornamental plants.

For consistent success, both amateur and professional breeders require detailed knowledge of the characteristics and history of a range of cultivars. The parents are chosen because of features that the breeder desires to pass to the offspring: scent, a particular colour or flower shape, health, vigour. In places with warm,

Opposite: Shrub rose 'Complicata' (see page 108)

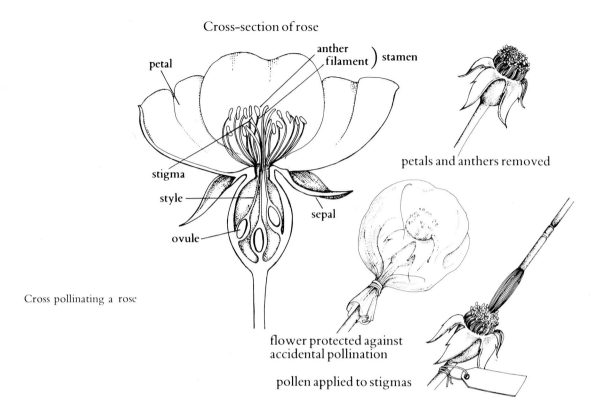

Cross-section of rose

petal

anther
filament) stamen

petals and anthers removed

stigma

style

sepal

ovule

Cross pollinating a rose

flower protected against
accidental pollination

pollen applied to stigmas

dry summers, pollination and seed ripening is possible in the open, but in higher latitudes a greenhouse is normally needed to give consistent results.

Fertilization is a highly complex sequence of events but it is a familiar biological one, so perhaps needs no fuller description here. To ensure that the chosen father is not upstaged, the flower that is selected to produce the seed is first emasculated by removing the anthers to prevent self-pollination. The petals are all taken off at the same time. In a greenhouse the insects that pollinate roses in nature can be excluded, but if there is any doubt the flower should be enclosed within a paper bag until deliberate pollination has taken place. This is done by dusting the pollen onto the stigma when it is receptive, which is shown when its surface appears moist or sticky. It can be touched with ripe anthers, or the pollen can be transferred by using a small brush or even a finger. The flowerheads should be labelled and protected until fertilization has taken place a few days later. Pollen can be stored for long periods if necessary, but it should be kept dry.

When the ripe fruits have been harvested they should be treated to break the dormancy of the seeds. The process is described elsewhere (see page 72); it can be accelerated by artificially regulating the temperature, maintaining a constant 21°C (70°F) for three months and then 0°C (32°F) for a further three months. Seed sowing is described in Chapter 6. After germination the seedlings are usually grown in a greenhouse until the first flowers appear. This occurs surprisingly early in their life. Plants that fail to show desirable characteristics are weeded out at this stage, and the remainder carefully assessed for the period they are in flower. The majority of seedlings generally prove to be worthless, and a large number in any batch are simply thrown away. Once the best seedlings have been selected they are budded so that they can be tested in the open, and the process of selection continued there.

Breeding a new cultivar is a painstaking task calling for skill and judgement, but it can be done by amateurs as well as professionals. Two very famous roses, 'Ena Harkness' and 'Frensham', were raised by Mr Albert Norman, who bred them and a number of other once esteemed cultivars in a small greenhouse in his garden.

SPORTS

New cultivars arise mostly as a result of deliberate breeding, but occasionally an existing rose produces a variant spontaneously. This is known as a sport, and if it has worthwhile characteristics that are different from those of its parent, it can be propagated vegetatively and thus produce a new cultivar. The most common examples of sports are the climbing types of bush roses, such as 'Climbing Elizabeth Harkness'. Sometimes a sport may take the form of a different colour – the yellow climbing rose 'Highfield' is a sport of 'Compassion', which is pink. Both cultivars have abundant, healthy, dark green leaves and a sweet scent.

CLASSIFICATION

The body responsible for classifying roses is the International Federation of Rose Societies. In 1979 it abandoned the old division between Hybrid Teas and Floribundas because the distinction had become blurred, and introduced two new groups instead. Large Flowered roses include those cultivars that carry their blooms singly, rather like the traditional Hybrid Teas. Cluster Flowered roses include most of the kinds that used to be called Floribundas. It is rather sad to see the old names disappear. They have served us well for a great many years and their inexplicability was part of that mystique with which gardeners like to bemuse their friends. The new names, being more or less self-explanatory, will make our art seem excessively simple.

The new groups are subdivided. Thus one has, for example, the snappy title of Dwarf Cluster Flowered Hybrids! Eventually the accretion of epithets in this way will make the names so unwieldy that they will be replaced, just as old botanical names composed of long descriptions were substituted by the present binomial system once Linnaeus had perfected it. Nurserymen are already starting the process. Patio Roses have now blossomed into catalogues, and the name seems very likely to stick. It is used in place of Dwarf Cluster Flowered Hybrids, and is a description not of the plant itself but of the place in which it might be used. For gardeners this is probably a good idea, just as the name shrub rose implies a place in a border, and bedding rose one in a flowerbed. The problem faced by the Federation is classification for show purposes, and for this it is necessary to group plants together because of their floral characteristics so that judges are only asked to compare like with like. I think we can safely assume that we have not heard the last word on the subject.

It is iconoclastic to say so, but the most useful classification for the general gardener is probably by colour, with subdivisions for height!

4
Cultivations

CHOICE OF SITE

Roses enjoy sunshine, but they may need some shade to allow the flowers a reasonable life in countries where sunlight and heat are intense. They prefer a well-drained site, and will not survive if there is stagnant water constantly around the roots. They are, however, tolerant about soil and will grow successfully in a wide range. Domestic gardens offer a variety of different aspects, and nearly all soils can be improved by compost and mulches. On wet sites drainage can be arranged by raising the beds above the surrounding levels so that surplus water can drain away, or, if an outlet for the water can be found, by installing a land drainage system.

The use of plastic drainpipes, which are perforated to admit water, makes drainage easier than it was when clay tiles had to be used. Drains should be laid systematically to a grid or herringbone pattern with a steady run of at least 1:200 towards the outlet. Steps should also be taken to improve the permeability of the soil by working in organic matter or grit, which will help the water to work its way downwards towards the drains.

If the site is exposed to strong winds some protection should be arranged, perhaps in the form of a fence or a planting scheme of tougher species to filter the wind. Draughty sites between houses should generally be avoided. In very dry places roses may find it difficult to grow, and they may be dwarfed or stunted as a result. Vigorous cultivars should be chosen to compensate for the difficult conditions.

Soil sickness is a condition that is little understood, but it is real enough. Roses usually become sickly in appearance and their growth will be stunted if they are planted in soil that has grown roses for many years. Nurserymen avoid the problem by rotating the crop. A private gardener faced with replacing worn-out rose bushes should look for a new location for the bed or change the topsoil for some that has not previously grown roses.

Once the site has been chosen it should be cultivated by digging and manuring, the rose bushes should be selected and planted, and routine cultivation can then take place. The following pages describe the work involved.

DIGGING

The purpose of digging soil is to bury surface weeds and debris, to allow manure and compost to be incorporated, to expose heavy soils to the action of frost which, particularly in the presence of lime, improves their structure, and to provide a friable surface in which planting can take place conveniently. Deep digging can improve drainage by breaking up hard pans of soil. This lets water drain through to more permeable earth below. A pan can be caused by repeated annual ploughing of agricultural land to a constant depth, and may be acquired along with a new house or garden. It can also be caused by heavy equipment

Opposite: Bush roses set off by climbers at The Royal Horticultural Society's garden at Wisley in Surrey

trailing over the site during construction. In these circumstances deep digging, also known as double digging, is justified, even though it is very laborious and time-consuming. As well as improving drainage it permits roots to penetrate more easily, thus increasing the drought resistance and stability of the plants. In other circumstances single digging is enough. This consists of turning the soil to the depth of a spade. The method is to open a trench the same width and depth as the spade, transferring the soil to the opposite end of the bed. If the bed is a wide one it can be divided in half longitudinally, a trench opened across one part and the soil transferred to the other. This saves a little labour. The soil is then turned systematically, burying compost and manure in each trench as work progresses. Perennial weeds should be removed entirely, but annual ones will simply rot away once they are turned upside down. Any turf should be chopped up in the bottom of the trench.

Digging is heavy work but it need not be back-breaking. There is no need to lift the soil high above the ground. It should be raised as little as possible and turned into the trench with a movement of the wrists. Nor should too much be taken on the spade at once. The work should be steady and rhythmic, done without strain.

Double digging involves breaking up the lower spit of soil as well as the top one, and working compost into it so that it is permanently improved. To permit this to be done a trench of three spade widths is made, the bottom dug with a fork or spade, manure or compost spread into it and then forked in. The next trench is dug by turning the soil into the open one and the process repeated. I have seen mountainous results from unskilled work, and it is necessary to do the job with attention to finished levels. The sides of the trenches should be kept vertical, the same width taken out each time, every spit should be turned to the full depth of the spade and the same amount of compost worked in each time, or the results will resemble a seismological disturbance of the earth's surface!

The surface of heavy soils should be left as rough as possible after digging so that frost and weather can work on them and improve their structure. If lime is required it should be applied at this stage, but it should not be brought into contact with manures or it will displace some of the plant nutrients they contain. When the time for planting arrives the bed should be trodden so that large air pockets are excluded, and a fork or rake used to produce a coarse tilth. Once this has been done fertilizer can be applied and planting can then proceed.

MANURING

Bush roses may remain for fifteen years or more in the same patch of ground, and shrub roses even longer. They make heavy demands on the soil for water and nutrients during this period, and everything possible should be done to improve soil fertility before planting. Using well-rotted organic matter is the best way of doing this, and it should be worked into the soil while it is being dug, though care is necessary when planting to prevent fresh manure from coming into contact with the roots.

In 1980 I reintroduced Clydesdale horses for cartage work in Aberdeen. We now have 22 working horses and they are used to do the same jobs previously done by light lorries. They have another great advantage for us. Each one produces manure to a value of £75 every year. It is not to be sniffed at! Any kind of manure is valuable. Horse manure is best on heavy soils, for it is open in texture and helps to counteract the natural density of the soil. It is now more frequently available as horses and ponies used for riding increase in number. Farmyard manure is the perfect material for lighter soils. In the middle of a city neither may be obtainable, or if they are they may be expensive so substitutes have to be found.

In some areas spent hops are available if a brewery is nearby. Their sharp, tangy smell is one of the abiding memories of my years at Wisley Gardens in Surrey, where large quantities were used to improve the very light, sandy soil. Garden compost is another useful material, and provided that the heap is properly made almost any item of organic origin – including newspapers, rags and straw as well as weeds, leaves and grass mowings – will rot down. Peat is also widely recommended, but it should be moist when it is used or it may subsequently remain dry and impervious to water and may do more harm than good. Old potting compost may also be available from nurseries on occasion, and is usually rich in residual nutrients as well as having a good texture and a high peat content.

Fertilizers can also be used with advantage. While mineral fertilizers give the best value for money, the traditional bonemeal is still popular, and because of its organic origin it can be applied in almost any amount without doing harm. It supplies phosphates, which stimulate root growth, and some nitrogen, which helps to develop strong foliage. These foods are released over a long period because the material decays relatively slowly in the soil. Compound fertilizers, which contain all the principal nutrients required for plant growth, are also used, and special rose fertilizers are also marketed. There is not much to choose between them, and if the soil has been well prepared I leave price to be the guide.

Whatever kind of fertilizer is used it can either be spread over the surface of a bed at about 25 g a square metre (1 oz per sq yd) and then raked in before planting takes place or, more economically, a small quantity may be dusted over the bottom of each planting hole, where the roots can easily reach it.

LIME

Roses are fairly tolerant about the degree of acidity of the soil, but like the great majority of plants seem to prefer a slightly acid one. However, the sweetly scented rambler rose 'Wedding Day' was produced at Highdown in the south of England in a garden that was once a chalk quarry.

Soil can be tested by readily available kits that use a chemical cocktail to react with the soil. The result is then compared with a colour chart, which gives an indication of the degree of acidity or alkalinity. This is measured on the pH scale: neutral soil has a pH factor of 7; readings higher than 7 are alkaline, those below 7 are acid. This is generally sufficient for gardeners, but the problem remains of how much hydrated lime, chalk or ground limestone to apply if the soil is very acid. These are the best forms of lime for garden use. In general the lighter and more sandy the soil, the less is needed to secure the required effect – up to 55 g of chalk per square metre (2 oz per sq yd) on the lightest soil is enough. If the soil is heavy, three or even four times this amount may be needed. On heavy soils lime applied in the autumn helps to coagulate the tiny particles of clay into crumbs, which improves the structure of the soil and permits air and water to pass through it more easily, to the great advantage of the roses. It also helps to release other plant foods, which are gripped in an Aberdonian grasp by the clay.

BUYING ROSES

Buying roses is comparatively easy. In many parts of the world they are even sold in department stores and supermarkets, as well as in garden shops and centres. The traditional way is to buy plants from a nursery, often as a result of reading a catalogue and sending an order through the post. Most nurseries will now also sell direct to visitors, so the customer has the opportunity to see and assess the choice of plants before making a purchase.

Specialist rose growers grade the plants they sell, and few of them will sell anything other than their top grade direct to the public. Sometimes second quality stock is sold off more cheaply, perhaps to a big buyer who does not mind waiting a year or so before getting the plants to their best. Using a reputable nursery is thus the best assurance of getting good quality stock, but even they vary one from another and it is worth knowing what to look for.

Large Flowered cluster rose 'Super Star' (see page 91)

Cluster Flowered bush rose 'Grandpa Dickson' (see page 92)

The traditional and still the most usual way of presenting plants for sale is with the roots exposed, except perhaps for a protective covering of polythene to stop them drying out, which they do when exposed to air. Desiccation kills tiny roots, and if carried too far will kill bigger ones as well. When this stage has been reached the whole plant is as good as dead and should be rejected by the purchaser. There should be at least three major roots arising close to the union (see page 44). They should be strong and well branched with plenty of fibrous roots, and they should be moist, not dried out. Any roots that have been damaged or broken when the plants were lifted should have been trimmed back to sound tissue with a clean cut straight across them. Suckers should have been pulled away. The stem into which the buds were inserted should be sturdy; if it is thin and weak another plant should be chosen. All the other shoots should be plump, firm and ripe. If in doubt, squeeze them; if they are unripe they will be soft and will give way to the pressure. If they have been allowed to get too dry they will both look and feel withered. The stems should be about the thickness of a pencil, and will usually have been cut to a length of 20 cm (8 in) or so by the nurserymen. There should be at least two stems arising from the point of union between stock and stem (see page 44).

In a supermarket or store, roses are often sold packed into sealed plastic containers. Shops tend to be warm, and this sometimes starts the plants into growth that will be soft and unable to withstand the atmosphere in the open air. The plant will also be weakened by the effort of making new growth, which can take place only at the expense of moisture already in the stem. My advice is to reject these plants, no matter what the price, and if necessary to look elsewhere.

It is possible to sell roses with bare roots only when the plants are without leaves during the dormant season, which in most temperate climates is from October to March, though the exact period varies with the season and the country. Many cultivars refuse to drop their leaves in time to get an early start to sales in the autumn, so nurserymen sometimes accelerate the process. If the leaves are not removed they will continue to lose water, and as this comes from the tissue of the plant the stems and roots eventually wither. Dormancy can be extended by keeping the plants in a cool store, so extending the planting season further into the spring.

Very occasionally shrub and species roses are sold with the roots packed in soil or peat, the whole being surrounded by sacking or polythene. They have good powers of survival because the packing keeps the roots moist, but even so they should only be planted during the dormant season.

Container-grown roses are another matter. For a start they are generally much more expensive. Their only advantage is that they can be planted at any season because the whole root system is kept intact and can be moved in its entirety. The extra expense is only justified in spring and summer, when bare-rooted plants cannot be used, and only then if the patience of the gardener will not extend until the next normal planting season in the autumn. It is important that the rose should genuinely be growing in the container, not just pushed into it for the sake of the sale, or all the advantages are lost. Plants should have been potted no later than early March, and by the time of sale should have made new fibrous roots, some of which should already have reached the bottom of the pot and may be starting to find their way through the drainage holes in search of moisture beyond. It is worth looking for these roots, as their presence is evidence that the plant is genuinely growing in the container. The branches should be well balanced and strong, free from pests and diseases and with dark, healthy leaves and vigorous shoots.

Even though the use of containers permits planting to take place in the growing season, a good deal of care is necessary to get the plants to establish themselves thereafter. They will certainly need to be watered in dry spells, and may need to be sprayed overhead once the sun has declined in the evenings. It is possible to give them artificial assistance by the use of one of the clear plastic transplanting sprays, which can be used to cover the leaves and shoots with a protective film that will reduce water loss while the roots are establishing themselves.

Climbing roses should be sold with longer stems, especially the climbing forms of bush roses, which if they are cut too hard are quite likely to revert to their old habits of growth. The stems should be at least 45 cm (18 in) long. Other climbers and ramblers should have stems at least 35 cm (14 in) long.

Standard roses should have vigorous, sturdy, straight stems that have been budded at the top with at least two buds reasonably close together. These are usually put on opposite sides so as to produce a well-balanced head composed of at least three and preferably more strong shoots. Full standards should have stems at least 1 m (40 in) long, half standards about 80 cm (36 in). Weeping standards should be grown on even taller stems so that their trailing shoots have plenty of scope to grow. It is possible to get them as tall as 1.8 m (6 ft) high.

PLANTING SEASON

Roses can be planted at any time that they are dormant, and in Europe this is usually between November and March depending on the particular season and the place. For example, in Aberdeen, Scotland it is often possible to continue planting throughout April and even into early May because growth starts late in the north. Further south it may be in full swing by February, and the planting season needs to be adjusted accordingly. There are parts of the world where growth hardly stops or does not stop at all; in these places roses are best grown in containers so they can be planted at any time. It must be said, however, that they are not well adapted to these climates and need a lot of care, including shading during the day.

In temperate regions autumn planting is best, because the soil is generally in good condition, being moist without being saturated and still warm from the sun. Roots soon become established in these conditions, and permit the plant to grow away quickly the following spring.

HEELING IN

If roses arrive before the ground is ready or when conditions make planting impossible, they should be laid close together in a trench. The roots are then covered with earth, which is pressed down onto them so that they remain moist and secure until the plants are required. The process is known as heeling in, and if it is done properly the plants can be stored for weeks without coming to harm. If the ground is hard with frost when the plants arrive they should be kept in a cool shed until they can be heeled in or planted, assuming that they have been properly packed. The main requirement is that the roots should be kept moist. If the plants have to be stored for more than a few days the packaging should be opened to permit air to circulate around the stems so that they do not heat up.

PLANTING DISTANCE

I prefer closer planting than is sometimes recommended. It is more expensive, of course, because more plants are required for a given area, but it does have the advantage of giving a more immediate effect once growth begins, and ensures an uninterrupted mass of colour when the plants start to flower. If they are too far apart the stems of neighbouring plants may never meet, and the display will be a rather patchy affair.

Distances between the plants should be varied depending on the vigour and habit of growth of the particular cultivar. Most medium-sized kinds can be planted successfully at 45 cm (18 in) apart, more vigorous cultivars at 60 cm (2 ft), smaller ones at proportionately less, down to the miniatures, which also vary in size, the bigger ones needing 30 cm (1 ft) between them and the smallest only 15 cm (6 in). These are probably only grown to advantage in a trough, window box or other container, and possibly in a rock garden. Shrub roses vary so much in size that each kind requires a different spacing. They should not, however, be set further apart than their ultimate spread.

When the roses abut a pathway or the edge of a lawn, the bushes should be put at least half the planting distance away from it or the stems will become a nuisance once they grow, catching the clothing of innocent passers by and getting in the way of mowing machines. Arranging the plants within the bed requires skill because it is desirable that they should be evenly spaced without looking regimented. They should not be planted in exact lines, and the bushes in one row should be planted so that they alternate with those in the next.

It is a good idea to mark out the positions the roses are to occupy before planting starts. This can be done by notching out the places with a spade or, more luxuriously, by using canes to identify each position. There is nothing more exasperating than to plant a bed and find at the end that two or three more roses are needed to complete it, the only remedies being another trip to the nursery – with the doubt hanging over the journey that the cultivars will have been sold out – or lifting the bushes and starting the planting process all over again.

The distance at which bushes are planted varies according to the climate. In the northern United States of America, for example, the spacing recommended here is suitable, but it should be increased by a quarter in warmer areas, and by half in states such as California and Florida, where the plants can grow to the maximum of their potential.

PREPARING THE PLANTS

Before planting, roses should be made ready by cutting back damaged roots to sound tissue if this has not already been done in the nursery. The cut should be square across the root, and made with a sharp knife or secateurs so that the tissue can heal rapidly. Very long roots should also be pruned so that the plant is easier to deal with.

Steep plants in water for 24 hours if they are dry on arrival

Cluster Flowered bush rose, 'Just Joey' (see page 92)

Normally the top growth will have been cut back to about half its length in the nursery. In the autumn and early winter further pruning should be left until the usual time, apart from cutting away any dead wood or stems that have been damaged in transit. If you have got the plants from a neighbour or propagated them yourself, or if you bought them from a nursery that has not bothered to trim them, the stems should be cut to about half their length before planting. This makes them easier to handle and reduces the risk of their being rocked and disturbed by the wind before the roots have got a grip of the soil. Any suckers should also be pulled away.

If the roots are dry the whole plant should be steeped in water for 24 hours, and even if they are not they should be stood in water for an hour or two before planting. The roots should then be kept covered with plastic or sacking to prevent them from drying out again while they are waiting to be planted.

Container-grown plants should also be soaked a day before planting so that all the soil is saturated. It is very difficult to wet the root ball afterwards if it was dry at the time of planting, and the growth will look sick and will become stunted. If a container plant is genuine, the root ball will be firm and well knitted together by a network of fibrous roots, and provided that the container is removed with care the root system will remain intact and can be planted in its entirety. The plant will then keep on growing unchecked. Most containers are not worth keeping for reuse, and they can be cut away so that the roots remain completely undisturbed. If a better quality pot has been used, tapping the rim with a spade or a large stone two or three times should be enough to release the plant.

PLANTING

Planting a bush rose
1 Prepare a planting hole large enough to accommodate all the roots; **2** Fill in the hole with fine soil; **3** Firm down the soil as you go; **4** The final soil level is about 2.5 cm (1 in) above the union of stock and scion

Planting should never be done when the soil is soaking wet. If it is worked in this condition the structure will be destroyed, and the surface will be puddled when the plant is firmed into place. This excludes air, which is essential for the roots, and makes it very difficult later on for rain to percolate down to them. On very light soils with a high content of sand there is much less risk of damage.

When the soil is frozen, planting should also be delayed until better conditions come along. Of course, if it is thoroughly hard planting is impossible anyway, but when only the surface is frozen it may be physically possible to plant, though it is undesirable. Frozen soil remains cold and hard for weeks if it is buried, and will check growth. In planting it is necessary for the roots and soil to be in close contact, and this is impossible if some of the soil is frozen into lumps.

The planting hole should be big enough to accommodate all the roots without cramping. One of the most common faults is to make it too small, so the roots have to be squashed and bent to get them into it. The hole should be deep enough to allow the plant to be placed a little lower than it was in the nursery. The level is

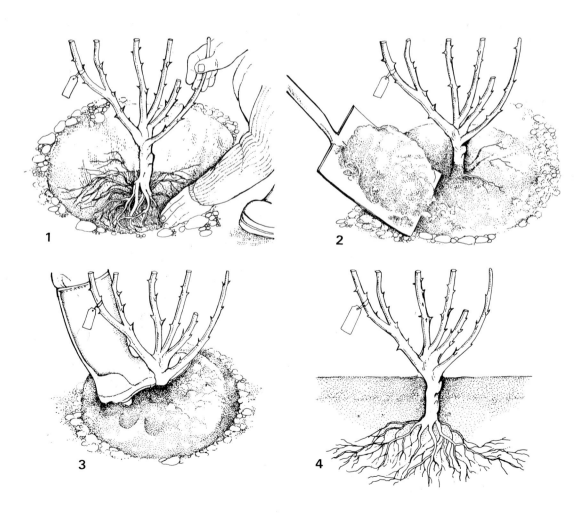

usually easy to see because of the change in colour of the bark. This should result in the union between the stock and scion being about 2.5 cm (1 in) below the surface of the soil. Some settlement takes place after planting, and the junction will eventually be at or immediately below ground level, which is the best place for it.

Once the hole has been dug the plant should be put into it, the roots spread out so that they occupy their natural positions, and the earth put back. Fine soil should be placed over the roots and the plant gently shaken up and down so that soil and roots are close together. When enough soil is in place it should be pressed down with the heel so that the plant is held firmly in place. This is partly to secure the plant in position and partly to make sure that the fibrous roots are pressed tightly into the soil so that they can absorb moisture from it. After this the hole should be filled to the level of the rest of the bed, the soil firmed again, and the surface loosened with a fork so that air and moisture can penetrate easily and footprints, which look unsightly if allowed to remain, are removed.

Standard roses need stakes to support them. These should be put into place, and hammered down until they are secure, after the hole has been dug but before the plant is put in. The stem should then be placed as close as possible to the stake, after which planting can proceed in the usual way.

The top of the stake should be cut off just below the head of growth and the stem tied to it, preferably using plastic ties that have a pad to prevent the bark being chafed when the plant moves in the wind. Tall standards should be tied in two places, once at the top and again towards the bottom. Ties should be checked each year, and adjusted when necessary to accommodate the expansion of the stem. Standards should preferably be staked for life to avoid the risk of damage in gales, so the stakes should be treated with preservative. In very severe climates standards are sometimes lowered to ground level to protect them in winter, and space should be allowed for this.

Standard roses need support
Below left: Hammer in the stake after the hole has been dug but before planting **Below:** Use tree ties to attach stem to stake and ensure head of standard does not chafe against the support.

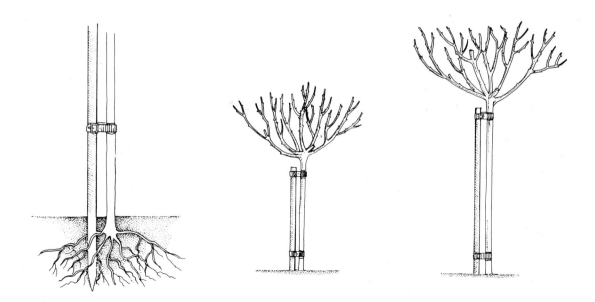

Opposite: One of the joys of summer – a window framed by a climbing rose
Left: The popular rambler 'Albertine' trained over a stone balustrade

Climbers have to be grown against a support of some kind. If this is a pillar or pergola the plant should be put as close to it as possible. If it is to grow against a wall it should be planted about 30 cm (1 ft) away so that the roots can pick up moisture more easily in the early stages. Eventually they will explore for moisture and nutrients, and a half-circle of soil about 1.2 m (4 ft) across should be dug and enriched with compost and manure before planting.

Spring maintenance

Severe frost loosens the soil and weakens the hold of recently planted bushes. They should be firmed back into place in the spring.

Immediately after pruning (see page 55 ff.) has taken place fertilizer can be sprinkled around the bushes, at the rate of 55 g per square metre (2 oz per sq yd). A compound fertilizer is suitable; I use a kind that has trace elements added to it. These are required by the plant in tiny amounts, and it used to be said that they were plentifully available so that applying them artificially was not necessary. Opinions change, however, and many growers now like to include them as well as nitrogen, to stimulate growth and the formation of dark healthy leaves, phosphate for root development, and potash to encourage flowering and later in the year to help the stems to ripen. Bonemeal, which is a horticultural feed-all, is often also used, though it contains a limited range of nutrients. Specialist formulations are also available.

Once fertilizer has been applied the surface of the soil should be loosened to let in air and water and to remove footprints. Only the top inch or two should be disturbed. There is no advantage in deep cultivation, and it can do harm by stimulating the growth of suckers and by disturbing the network of roots that roses develop quite close to the surface.

If weedkillers are to be used they should be applied at this stage (see page 48), or a mulch may be used to keep weeds down. Peat, bark, and well-made compost are sterile and will not develop a crop of weeds of their own, but other materials, such as manure or compost that has not been stacked properly, can be treated with weedkiller once they have been spread to prevent the growth of seedling weeds. Grass mowings are very useful for mulching, though if the lawn has recently been treated with selective weedkillers they should not be used among roses.

Weedkilling

On a small scale a hoe is the best weedkiller, if it is used regularly on dry days when the weeds can be desiccated before they get a chance to send their roots down into the soil again. A Dutch hoe, which is the kind that is pushed, is the best for use in a rose bed as it is usually possible to reach all parts of the soil surface from the surrounding paths or lawns. Hoes should be kept sharp, so they glide through the soil easily without too much effort and cut the weeds just below ground level. Provided that perennial weeds are removed before planting and the hoeing is regular enough to stop other weeds from producing seed, the soil can be kept acceptably clean by hoeing alone.

On a large scale weedkillers may be needed, and there are several to choose from. The one that I use, after several flirtations with other chemicals, is simazine. It is available under a variety of proprietary names. Used at low concentrations (at higher ones it will kill almost everything) it will prevent the germination of seeds and thus keep the ground clear. It will not kill perennials, so these should be removed in their entirety; nor will it kill plants that are already growing, so it should be applied to bare earth as soon as pruning and any associated cultivation has taken place. Once the chemical has been applied the soil surface should be left undisturbed. It should not be used the first year after planting. Continual use of simazine among roses seems to do no harm to the plants themselves, but it does permit a green algal covering to develop over the soil, and the ground should be lightly forked each winter after pruning to get rid of it.

It is necessary to observe the manufacturers' instructions carefully for both the storage and the application of weedkillers, and especially to observe any safety precautions they recommend, including thorough cleaning of equipment before putting it to any other purpose.

Mulching

Mulching is desirable on nearly all soils and has several beneficial effects. It helps to keep the soil moist by absorbing rain and acting like a sponge to provide a cool root run, which roses like. It also suppresses most weeds except for well-established perennial ones, and the materials used eventually decay, providing plant foods and improving the surface soil.

Applying a mulch is an annual job that should be done only when the soil is thoroughly moist. In temperate climates the best time is in early spring, just after pruning. Care should be taken not to pile the material against the stems of the roses because it can damage the bark if it lies wet and cold against it. To be

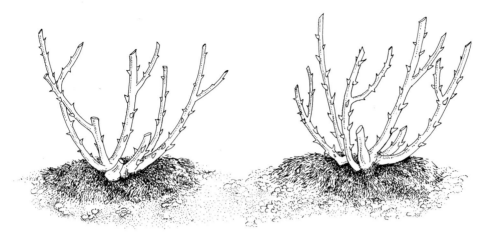

Mulch roses annually with well-rotted garden compost or manure. This will not only keep the soil moist but also keep down the weeds

effective the mulch should be at least 10 cm (4 in) deep. A variety of materials can be used. Organic ones, preferably sterile and free from weed seeds, are the best. Well-made compost, well-rotted manure, leafmould or lawn mowings are the better materials, though peat – which is expensive to use for the purpose – and, increasingly, pulverized bark are also possibilities. I have seen black polythene used effectively, and once the roses had grown it was almost invisible, though it was rather unsightly up to that time. If it is perforated it will let water through; otherwise it waterproofs the soil.

Mulches should be put on early, when the ground is still thoroughly wet from winter rains, and in the case of bark and other light materials when there is still the likelihood of more rain falling to settle it securely into place.

Other materials are used in different parts of the world. They include mushroom compost, wool shoddy, sugar cane refuse, buckwheat, cottonseed or peanut hulls and ground corn cobs. In practice, any easily available organic material will do. There are two conditions: it must eventually decay to form a useful component of the soil, and it must persist long enough on the surface to do its work as a mulch. If there is a choice of materials, the one with the best appearance should perhaps be selected.

Summer and autumn maintenance

In very dry climates roses need irrigation in the summer. There is a range of equipment for the purpose. I have seen water applied effectively by means of a trickle irrigation system, which applies it a drop at a time through a network of plastic tubes that visit each plant. The system is permanently in place and works continuously throughout the dry season, delivering water without waste to precisely where it is needed.

Plastic pipes that supply water through a series of nozzles and are also left permanently in position may be used, the water being applied in the evenings or at night, minimizing the loss that occurs as a result of evaporation. Enough water should be given to soak the soil to its full depth. Wetting the surface alone only makes matters worse, because the fine feeding roots move towards a water supply, and if attracted upwards become more vulnerable to drought. In northern Europe, where rain is fairly evenly distributed throughout the year, irrigation is not necessary except when container plants have been put in during late spring or summer, or in an extremely dry spring when newly planted bushes may need a little help to get started.

Pest and disease control may be necessary at intervals throughout the spring and summer (see page 75 ff). The rose grower should be vigilant during these seasons, and act quickly to suppress any attack.

Once flowering has finished, the dead blossoms should be removed in order to encourage a second crop, though shrub roses esteemed for the brightness of their hips should be left alone.

Roses are able to absorb nutrients through their leaves, and specially formulated foliar feeds are available to give the bushes an extra gloss in the summer months and to sustain vigorous, healthy growth. They can also be used on soils with a high lime content, from which the bushes may be unable to absorb all the nutrients they need. Several manufacturers make suitable compounds, which are sold in liquid form so they are easy to dilute and apply. They can also be mixed with the sprays used to control pests and diseases.

Opposite: *Rosa moyesii* (see page 108) has a second season of beauty when covered by decorative hips **Right:** The white patio rose 'Nozomi' (see page 101) and shrub rose 'The Fairy' (see page 112) with the Large Flowered bush rose 'Silver Jubilee' behind (see page 90)

Disbudding
produces a single
large bloom
suitable for
exhibition

In the autumn fallen leaves should be raked up, removed and preferably burned, as they can harbour the overwintering stages of pests and diseases. On very exposed sites autumn pruning will help the plant to withstand the effect of strong winter winds. After that the plants can be left to their own devices until pruning time comes round again, except in very severe climates where winter protection is needed, for example by laying fir branches or straw over the beds to mitigate the effects of extreme frosts.

A deep covering of snow will add to the protection, but if this cannot be relied on, or in places with very severe winters, the bases of the plants should be covered with a mound of dry soil heaped among the stems up to 30 cm (1 ft) high before the ground freezes. The object is to conduct such warmth as there is in the earth upwards into the heap. Once there has been enough frost to harden the surface, the heaps can be mulched with straw or dry, loose leaves to slow down heat loss. This work should not be done too soon or it will create desirable winter homes for rodents.

In still colder climates this treatment may not be enough. The plants can be dug up and buried about a metre deep, but the effort involved makes this impractical. Covering the plants with a box is sometimes recommended. It should be 50 cm (20 in) high and big enough to protect several neighbouring plants. Once in place it can be filled with insulating material and covered with polythene to keep the contents dry.

Climbing plants should be lowered to ground level and protected in the same way. Each stem may have to be untied and dealt with separately; a better way is to support them on a trellis hinged at the base so that both can be lowered together.

Standards can also be lowered to the ground and protected, or grown in wire baskets to make lifting and handling easier. They can then be moved in the autumn to a cool cellar or shed until better weather returns.

EXHIBITION ROSES

Gardeners who wish to exhibit roses in flower shows have a slightly different regime to follow because for them perfect foliage and flowers are essential. Disbudding (see opposite) not only produces bigger individual flowers, it can also be used as a method of timing them so that they reach their best stage at show time. The earlier the unwanted buds are removed, the earlier the remainder will develop, and the converse is also true. Three or four times the number of roses actually needed for the exhibit should be prepared so that there will be a good selection to choose from. Only the best should be sent to a show; gold medals are seductive and winning them should be the aim of every exhibitor.

The blossoms of large flowered cultivars need to be protected from the effects of adverse weather as soon as the buds start to show colour. A polythene bag, with perforations to prevent condensation and supported over a wire frame to give the flower plenty of room to expand, can be used. When the roses are picked the thorns should be removed so they will not rip the foliage when the flowers are in transit. The stems should be steeped up to their necks in water in a cool place for several hours after cutting so that the flowers arrive at the show in the best possible condition.

Exhibits can also be doctored a little to improve on nature. If they have powdery traces of mildew the evidence can be wiped away; aphids can also be removed at this stage. If the surfaces of leaves are to be visible at the show they may be given an extra gloss by the use of one of the oil-based materials sold to give a polished look to house plants; wiping them with full cream milk gives nearly the same effect.

Irredeemably defective petals on the outside of the flower can be eased away. This should be done gently so they leave no jagged tell-tale residue. Flowers also respond to a little massage to get them into perfect shape. Outer petals may be gently enticed into position, and even the centre can sometimes be opened slightly by blowing into it. My last piece of advice on the subject is to make sure that the rules of the particular class are followed exactly. Judges are conformists, and their first job is to make sure that exhibits exactly match the stipulations in the show schedule. There are various specialist publications that offer advice on how best to select, prepare and exhibit roses in competitions.

If you grow roses and are within reach of a suitable flower show it is well worth exhibiting, and it is not as difficult as the outsider sometimes supposes. Rose societies in many countries run important shows of their own, where competition is keen and the highest standards are often attained. They are worth entering even for a beginner. Shows bring contact with leading growers, act as forums and set standards of excellence.

5
Pruning

REASONS FOR PRUNING

A work study expert looking at the practices of rose growers would first of all enquire why pruning is bothered with at all. Most shrub roses grow perfectly well without elaborate attention, and some bush roses are also vigorous enough to grow without pruning.

Left alone, however, the lower stems of bush roses become hard and unproductive and look ugly. They also produce a cluster of crowded shoots from the younger wood at the top. This makes the bush unstable in wind because of the leverage that is exerted on the roots. Eventually the stems die, and may have no young basal growths to replace them so that the life of the bush itself may be shortened. When shoots are crowded sunlight cannot reach them, and as a result they have difficulty in ripening as they should in late summer and autumn, and become vulnerable to damage by frost. Crowded stems discourage air movement, creating conditions that encourage the spread of diseases such as black spot. The flowering of many cultivars is also impaired.

Pruning ensures a good supply of vigorous shoots that arise from somewhere near the base of the plant. The whole bush will then be clothed with leaves throughout the growing season. It lets in light so the stems ripen better, pest and disease control is easier, the bushes are more stable in wind, and the flowers are bigger and are produced at a height at which they can be enjoyed.

Pruning can also be used to produce a better shaped, more balanced bush. Stems start to grow in the same direction that the bud faces, so pruning to an outward-facing bud helps to keep the centre of a bush uncluttered. It is also possible to direct growth inwards, as may be required when a shoot is close to a path or a sprawling variety needs to be encouraged to grow upwards.

As many as three buds often develop and take their own directions, but the top one generally grows first, usually produces the most vigorous shoots and remains dominant thereafter.

ANNUAL PRUNING

The aim of pruning is to produce a well-shaped bush with an open centre and plenty of strong, well-spaced shoots arising as near ground level as possible. Of course this ideal is not always attained; pruning is generally a matter of compromise and doing the best with the material available.

The first job is to remove all the dead wood, which should be cut right back to the base. If the plant is vigorous and has plenty of shoots to choose from, the weakest stems should also be cut away entirely. Once this has been done the shape of the bush will have become clearer and pruning proper can begin.

If larger and fewer flowers are required, perhaps for showing, then pruning should be hard and involves cutting all the growths to within three buds of their base. The same severe treatment should be given to newly planted bush roses so

Opposite: Roses need not be grown on their own. They also play a valuable role in the mixed border with other flowering shrubs and perennials such as *Alchemilla mollis*

that the top growth is in balance with the root system, a large part of which will have been damaged and left behind, no matter how carefully it has been lifted in the nursery. Plants that are weak should also be cut back in the same way, as severe pruning encourages the vigorous growth of new stems.

After a very cold winter there may be no choice but hard pruning, because the stems may have been so badly frozen that the only healthy wood is right at the base. It is necessary to find this wood, as the stems will otherwise try to do so spontaneously by dying back to it or even beyond. It is possible to tell whether the stem has been damaged or not by the colour of the soft central tissue, known as the pith. It is normally white, but injury by frost turns it brown or grey. The state of the outer layers is not a sufficient indication by itself as they may appear healthy long after the pith is dead. If it has not ripened properly in the autumn the pith will look granular and the stem will also die back, and should therefore be removed.

Most of us want a good show of blossom from rose bushes to decorate the garden. To secure this effect, lighter pruning is done by taking the stems back to about six inches from the base. This also has the happy effect of letting the bush flower a week or so earlier.

Pruning a bush rose
1 First remove any old or dead wood; **2** Thin out the centre to produce a well-balanced open shape; **3** Hard prune for large blooms or after a very cold winter when growth can be damaged by frost; **4** Alternatively a lighter pruning will give a good display of flowers; **5** Always prune to just above an outward facing bud and make sure the cut slopes away from this to shed water

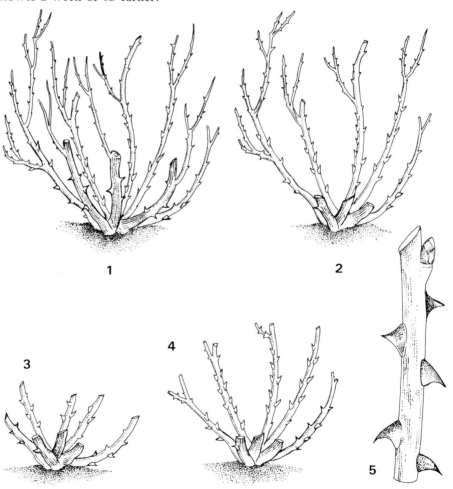

When pruning, the stem should be cut at a slight angle so as to shed water. The cut should be just above a bud, because at this point healing can take place and the new shoot will emerge. Care should be taken not to damage the bud, or of course it will not grow. The cut should be well clear at about 0.5 cm ($\frac{1}{4}$ in) above, and sloping downwards and away from the bud.

Luckily roses are able to endure hardships and one season's bad pruning is unlikely to kill them, so the grower has a chance to assess the effect of what he has done and make the necessary adjustments the following year.

WHEN TO PRUNE

The time to prune roses varies across the world, as you might expect. In some climates there is no dormant season, as there is in more northerly and southerly places, so roses have to be pruned between spells of flowering, though the same principles apply as elsewhere. I live in one of the most northerly cities in the world and prefer to prune roses in March, as soon as the weather starts to improve and just as the sap is beginning to rise. Further south, where spring comes earlier, the plants may be ready to prune in late February depending on the weather. In general, the lower the latitude, the earlier the work can be done. If only a few bushes are involved it is best to choose a mild day, when it is pleasant to be in the garden and the job can be tackled systematically until it is completed. If a lot of roses have to be pruned the work may have to be done over a period, and that may mean starting a little earlier in the year than is ideal and finishing later. If the work is done too early the wounds will not start to heal at once, and will remain vulnerable to infection and rot and be exposed to penetration by rain and subsequent damage by frost. If it is done too late, the plant will have wasted its energy in producing shoots that are then cut away, the cut stem will also bleed and although the problem is not really very severe on roses, it is nevertheless a check to growth.

I sometimes still hear autumn pruning being recommended. At one time it was the subject of much controversy. As most of my own gardening has been done in comparatively severe climates, I have no doubt that the best time is March, perhaps earlier if the spring arrives prematurely and later if the winter is long.

There is one situation in which light pruning in the autumn is justified, however, and that is when the bushes are exposed to winds and gales. Shortening the stems by cutting them in the late autumn to about half their height reduces the amount of growth upon which the wind can exert pressure. Without pruning the bushes may be rocked to and fro in strong winds, the roots will become loosened, and on heavy soil the movement will create a cup of compressed soil around the base of the stem in which water can collect and cause damage, particularly if it freezes.

EQUIPMENT FOR PRUNING

I started work with a head gardener who had deeply held convictions about pruning. He insisted that it should be done with a pruning knife, and one of these, with a strong, hooked blade, was my first gardening purchase. My hands bear

The dainty shrub rose 'Ballerina' (see page 108)

the scars of it to this very day, because if they are to be effective knives must be kept razor sharp, and they are likely to involve the less skilful user in much bloodshed. As soon as I was removed from this forceful superintendance I acquired a pair of secateurs, which do the same job almost as well. The preference for a knife was in theory well founded, because if it is kept very sharp it makes a clean cut without tearing or bruising the plant, so the wound heals rapidly. A badly pruned stem takes much longer, or may never heal at all and then will die back.

If you are choosing a knife buy one with good quality steel that can be honed to perfect sharpness and that will retain its edge. Lacerations can be made to soft human flesh by a poor cheap blade as easily as by a better quality, more expensive one, but the roses will notice the difference.

Secateurs, like knives, must be kept sharp. Failure to do this is one of the most common causes of bad pruning. They should be taken apart to be sharpened so that the job can be done thoroughly. One side of the blade is flat, and this should not be touched; the other side is chamfered, and is the one to work on. A fine carborundum stone lubricated with a few drops of oil or water should be used. The blade should first be cleaned with a kitchen scourer to remove dirt and dried sap. It should then be rotated over the stone at the same angle as the existing cutting edge and pressed down by the forefinger. The blade should be checked regularly, and when it is thoroughly sharp should be turned upside down and pressed flat against the stone to smooth away any burring on the other side. It is of course possible simply to open the secateurs and rub the stone over the blades without taking them apart, but this is awkward to do and the result is inferior. Sharpening should be done regularly during pruning because the blades soon get blunt.

There are several designs of secateurs but there are three principal groups. The first are those with curved blades that operate rather like a pair of scissors. Only the convex blade is kept sharp; it cuts against the squared edge of the concave blade. The second group has only one blade, which operates by pressing the stem against a flat anvil. The cut is complete when blade and anvil meet, so not only sharpness but also accurate setting is necessary. There are several variations on this type. One of them has a ratchet, which enables the pressure to be built up in a series of movements, and is useful for people who cannot grip very well. The third group is the 'parrot bill' secateurs. One blade is completely concave and the other partly so; both are kept sharp.

It is worth taking trouble over choosing a pair of secateurs. They differ from one another in important matters such as weight and balance as well as in price. It is desirable to get a pair that suits you personally. An overall length of 22 cm (8 in) is fine for most people, but the handles of some may open too wide to be comfortable for people with small hands. The spring should be strong enough to return the blades to an open position without an exasperating delay once a cut has been made, and they should not require a major exertion to close them.

A single bush may need 15 or more pruning cuts. Badly designed secateurs and excessively strong springs needlessly add to the work. Secateurs should have strong, easily reached safety catches that can be pushed into place by the thumb of the hand that holds them. Left-handed people will find the catch is not quite so easy to use because most brands of secateurs are made with right-handed people in mind. At least one manufacturer has a left-handed design, however, and given the frequency with which secateurs are used it is worth taking trouble to find a design that is entirely suitable. Spare parts, such as secateur springs, should also be easy to obtain for the model you select.

When using secateurs a single, clean cut should be made. They should never be twisted or wrenched in order to get through a stem, and if this is necessary a pruning saw or a pair of lopping shears should be used instead. The shears are to all intents and purposes secateurs with extra big, strong blades and with long handles that allow much greater leverage to be exerted. You may be glad to have a pair handy when pruning big shrub roses, or even ramblers, because they have the additional advantage of keeping the operator at a distance from the potential discomfort of contact with prickly stems.

For even larger stems, a pruning saw is a great help. It too should be kept sharp, though saw sharpening is really a professional job, and even then the wound may need to be pared with a sharp knife to expose unchafed tissue that can make the quickest recovery. There are two main designs. One has a straight blade, and teeth on both sides, the other has a curved blade with the teeth on one side only. I prefer the latter type because it is easier to get it into confined and awkward places.

Perhaps it goes without saying that a pair of strong leather gloves is also a fundamental piece of equipment for a pruner of roses. I use a pair of gauntlet gloves, which protect my wrists and reduce the likelihood of stray detached prickles finding their way inside.

SUCKERS

The majority of roses are propagated in nurseries by means of budding. This means that two different, though closely related, plants are united to form one. The part that supplies the roots is called the stock; this is always a species or variety that can be produced easily from seed. There are several in use, but none of them is worth a place in a garden in their own right. For example, one of the most common is the dog rose. The bud of the cultivar is inserted at the very base of the stem of the stock, and once it grows the rest of the plant is cut back to a point just above it. A short portion of the original stem remains, and this is sufficient to produce new shoots occasionally, at or just below ground level. These are known as suckers.

A sucker can be recognized partly because it comes from below the other stems and also because the colour, shape and conformation of the leaf is different from that of the cultivar itself. Much depends on the stock that the nurseryman used. The dog rose is fairly easy to recognize: its leaflets are narrower, smaller and paler in colour than most garden cultivars. Other stocks are not so distinct, but even these can be picked out by comparing their characteristics with those of the cultivar.

In tearing out suckers it is important to leave the strong, vigorous, reddish-coloured shoots of the cultivars, which often also thrust upwards from near the bottom of the plant, and which help to keep the bush growing healthily from the base. Difficult growing conditions may sometimes stimulate the plant into producing suckers; for example, deep cultivation too close to the plants or a frost severe enough to injure the top growth.

Suckers should be removed as soon as they are noticed.
Right: Scrape away the soil around a bush rose to find the point of origin.
Far right: Pull off any suckers from the stem of a standard rose

Suckers can be a great nuisance on roses, and it is essential to be on the alert and to remove them as soon as they start to grow. They are easiest to deal with when they are young and soft and can simply be rubbed away with a gloved hand. They have first call on the water supply of the plant, so they grow rapidly once they start and soon become dominant. They starve and eventually smother the top growth if they are left for more than a year or two, and a knowing neighbour will then no doubt tell you that the bush has gone wild. If a sucker does become established it should not be pruned, as this would leave enough buds behind to allow it to send out new shoots. It should be pulled away so that a heel at the base is removed as well, thus ensuring that nothing will grow from the same point again.

The best method is to scrape a little soil from the base of the rose until the place where the sucker started can be seen. One foot should be placed close to the bush to prevent the roots being loosened when the sucker is removed. The sucker should be grasped at the base and pulled sharply downwards. The soil should then be put back and heeled into place.

SHRUB ROSES

Shrub roses differ a good deal in treatment from the bush cultivars. They are more often grown on their own roots, so suckers are less of a problem, though the hybrids and cultivars of *Rosa rugosa* and *R. gallica*, among others, tend to be invasive, and their basal growths may well need to be removed to keep them within reasonable bounds. Many shrubs, like *R. moyesii*, naturally form a thicket of growth that only very occasionally needs heading back.

Those that are budded are not very likely to produce suckers unless the stock is exposed or injured by careless cultivation. When they do appear, suckers should be removed in the same way as in bush roses (see opposite).

Pruning after planting should be done by cutting the stems hard back to two or three buds from the base, so that vigorous new growth is encouraged from as close to the ground as possible and the activity of the roots, which will be temporarily reduced by transplanting, is balanced by a reduction in demand for water by the top growth.

Subsequent pruning of shrub roses depends on the species or cultivars concerned, though dead and straggly shoots should be cut out from all of them. Some, like *Rosa hugonis*, need no pruning beyond what is necessary to keep them within bounds. Among the others, a proportion of the oldest shoots can be cut back to the base after flowering so as to leave space for new wood to develop and ripen. It is from this growth that the best flowers will be produced the following year, and it also ensures a supply of young wood. Cultivars that produce handsome fruit should not be pruned until late winter.

Whenever it is done, the work can be awkward and painful, and the plant offers a powerful incentive to follow the classic advice that one should never prune officiously or without need. Any very vigorous, abnormally long growths that some cultivars occasionally develop should be cut back to the length of the other shoots or they will swing around in the wind, and unless the plant is well established may cause it to rock, producing a gap between the compacted soil and the stem in which water may lodge.

Rosa sericea var. *omeiensis* forma *pteracantha* (see page 113) is grown for its outsize coloured thorns rather than for its flowers

Rosa sericea var. *omeiensis* forma *pteracantha* (*R. omeiensis* forma *pteracantha*) is most esteemed for its large red prickles. These are at their best only for a year, after which they turn grey. Pruning this plant aims at a steady production of young growth from near the base, and the old shoots should all be cut down to ground level at the end of winter.

MINIATURES

Miniature roses need to be pruned in much the same way as their larger cousins. Weak and dead wood should be cut away, and the remaining growths shortened to about half their length. Occasionally tall, gawky shoots are produced, and these should be removed or they spoil the look of the plant.

STANDARD ROSES

Standards are usually budded onto stocks of *R. rugosa*, which form the stem right up to the point at which the flowering shoots arise. Suckers are thus very easy to pick out, both because of their easily seen point of origin and because of the distinctive dark foliage of the stock. They should be removed as soon as they appear.

Pruning follows the needs of the particular cultivar. The stem should be pruned to within four or five buds of the base, not cutting too hard as the object is to produce a graceful, full head of flowers exclusively for garden display. Weeping standards are a different matter, and should be pruned when blooming is over by cutting the stems that have carried the flowers right back to the base, retaining the young shoots for next year's crop. Most of them are rambler cultivars, which flower only once a year.

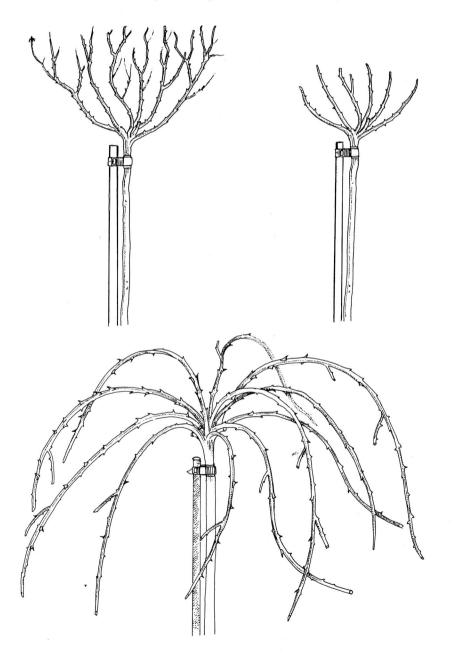

Prune a standard rose with care to promote a graceful head of flowers throughout the summer

Far left: before; **Left:** after

The young growths of a weeping standard are retained while those shoots that have flowered are cut right back

CLIMBERS AND RAMBLERS

Rose breeders have been busy improving climbing roses. The old divisions between them and ramblers are now blurred – if they were ever clear. As with all roses, it is necessary to observe the habit and characteristics of growth and to treat the plant accordingly.

Climbers mostly flower on side growths, often called laterals, which are produced from a framework of main stems. When flowering is over the laterals should all be cut back to within two or three buds of their base. Some produce a regular supply of new shoots from the bottom of the plant; these can be tied in to replace older, worn-out stems, which can then be cut away. In other cases old, unproductive wood can be pruned to a well-placed, strong lateral, which is then used in its place.

The old-fashioned rambler roses are less popular nowadays because they have a comparatively short flowering season. Cultivars like 'Dorothy Perkins' usually produce plenty of young growth from the base, and the old stems can be cut back as soon as flowering is over and replaced by the new ones. They are domestic in scale compared with ramblers like *Rosa filipes* 'Kiftsgate', which is a mammoth that will grow to 12 m (40 ft), and spread even wider than that. It has particularly aggressive prickles. Roses do not produce thorns in the strict botanical sense as these develop from the wood of the plant, whereas on a rose the weapons are developed from the epidermis and are called prickles, though this sounds like an unjustified diminutive. In the case of 'Kiftsgate' they are not numerous but are sharp enough to make pruning one of the most miserable jobs known to horticulture. Luckily the plant, like other very vigorous ramblers, does not need regular pruning – in fact its scale makes systematic pruning impracticable. Dead wood and straggling shoots that are wandering beyond their preferred limits should, however, be removed where possible.

A well pruned climbing rose should display a balanced and evenly-spaced framework. Train in new laterals and cut back old unproductive growths to a strong replacement. Other laterals that have flowered should be cut back to two or three buds

SUMMER PRUNING

Sometimes even skilled gardeners leave too much stem above a bud, or the stems may be bruised by badly set or blunt secateurs, or perhaps they are affected by a severe late frost. All these problems can cause them to die back, sometimes right to the base. It is just as well to cut dead wood out whenever it appears, or it looks unsightly, is a mute declaration of horticultural fault, and what is worse acts as a potential harbour for pests and diseases. Dead wood should be cut down to the nearest healthy bud, or if a shoot is completely dead to a point flush with the parent stem.

As soon as the flowers have been fertilized, the plant sets about seed formation. This uses up its energy and may even prevent a second show of blossom from being produced. The stems, with their burden of spent blossoms, should be cut at a place two leaves or so below the point of origin of the lowest flowers in order to encourage new growth. Old varieties or cultivars of shrub roses that do not produce a second crop should be left alone, as should species roses valued for the quality of their hips.

Disbudding (see page 52) is another form of summer pruning and on cultivars that produce large flowers is sometimes worth while when even bigger ones are required, perhaps for cut flowers or for exhibiting at a flower show. For garden decoration it is not necessary. The method is to remove all the side buds as soon as they are big enough to handle, retaining the central bud alone. It is also possible to obtain a more uniform head of flowers in cluster flowered cultivars by removing the central bud, which otherwise usually opens before the rest.

DISPOSAL

Getting rid of the prunings is an important consideration. They should preferably be burned, because they are potential resting places for pests and diseases and act as centres of infestation and infection if they are left about. In towns garden bonfires are not very neighbourly, and if the prunings cannot be burned they should be taken to a tip.

6
Propagation

Propagating plants at home is a source of great satisfaction. There are two principal methods by which roses are reproduced. Budding is still the chief way, and with some perseverance can be achieved in gardens; micropropagation requires elaborate facilities beyond the means of all but professional nurserymen. Other methods include cuttings, separation of rooted suckers, layering, and sowing seed, all of which can be tried by amateurs.

BUDDING

Budding is the nurseryman's traditional way of propagating a wide range of shrubs and trees, including roses. It is a form of grafting and allows the favourable characteristics of two plants to be combined into one. Thus the root system, called the stock, is provided by a plant that is easy to propagate, vigorous, tough and disease resistant. The top growth, or scion, is supplied by the decorative cultivar esteemed for its blossom and perhaps for its foliage.

Budding has other merits as well. It allows a large number of plants to be produced from comparatively little scion material, which is important when a new cultivar is being bulked up for sale. It produces a saleable plant in little more than a year: roses budded in the summer will be available for sale from the autumn of the following year. Using the right stock evens out the differences in vigour between cultivars and allows plants to be produced with reliable root systems, tough enough to grow in most gardens and resistant to the trauma of lifting, packing and travel. The method is also comparatively cheap, as the stocks are capable of being produced quickly in large numbers and can be lifted and planted again by machines.

A skilled craftsman can do his work at a surprising rate. Contract budders who move between nurseries are capable of putting in several thousand buds a day, with an assistant following behind tying the buds into place. Even this job has been transformed by new materials, which permit the fastenings to be clipped on whereas before they had to be made with wet raffia.

In the confines of a garden there are several restrictions, of which the most important is the problem of obtaining stocks. These can be purchased from specialist growers, but normally only in large quantities, though a nurseryman may possibly let a customer buy a more manageable number. Some stocks, for example *Rosa rugosa*, can be propagated in the garden by using cuttings; seeds can sometimes be sown, as in the case of the common briar, *R. canina*.

A variety of stocks is used. The current selections are very much better than those they have replaced, being less prone to suckering and more uniform in growth. Home gardeners may have to take what they can get, but if there is a choice the better ones include 'Pfänders', *inermis*, *manettii* or 'Laxa'. *Rosa rugosa*, which can be raised from cuttings, is also used for standards; the hybrid 'Hollandica' is superior to the type.

Opposite: Shrub rose 'Nevada' (see page 114)

Budding to create
a new bush rose:
1 Take a bud;
2 Remove the
wood from behind
the bud if
necessary; **3** Make
a T-cut in the stem
of the stock;
4 Insert the bud in
the T-cut; **5** Tie
the bud in place
with raffia so it can
knit together with
the tissues of the
stock

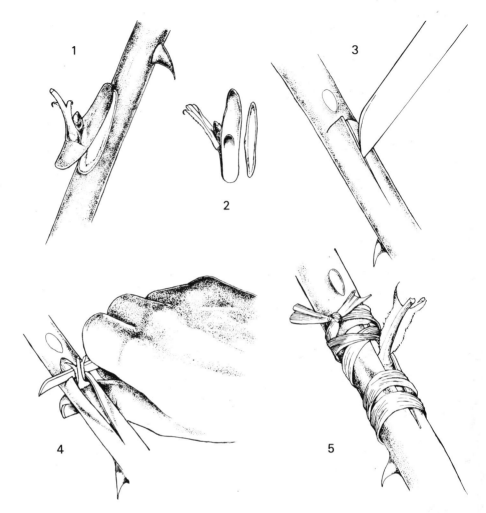

Seedling root stocks are grown for a season, after which they are graded and sold. By the time they are budded, the stem base should be about as thick as a pencil. They should be planted when dormant. In a garden they can be put in rows 1 m (3 ft) apart with about 30 cm (1 ft) between them. They should be planted shallowly, with a little of the root protruding above ground level to make budding easier. This portion and the base of the stem should be covered with soil after planting to keep the bark soft and moist. The soil is cleared away to expose the stem just prior to budding.

The time of budding varies depending on the season and the location. In higher latitudes the plants are generally ready between mid and late summer. The stocks must be well established, big enough to accommodate the bud, the plants actively growing and with bark that lifts easily. If the job is attempted too early or too late, the bark sticks tight to the wood and budding is impossible. The scion wood must also be available, and have fully developed, healthy buds. It is cut into lengths by removing the leaves and the soft upper parts of the shoots, leaving a short length of stalk to act as a handle. The prickles should also be removed for ease of handling. The best buds are to be found in the middle of the shoot, and bud sticks are usually about a foot long when prepared. After preparation they should be kept cool and moist until they are used, though the sooner budding takes place the better.

To prepare the bud is the work of seconds for professionals but is a much slower job for a gardener propagating only a few plants. A sharp knife is used, preferably one of the various designs of budding knife. This is inserted into the bark about 1 cm ($\frac{2}{5}$ in) below the bud. A cut is then made to about the same distance on the other side, bringing the blade to the surface and pulling away the bark, which is then trimmed about 1 cm ($\frac{2}{5}$ in) from the bud. Some wood will still be attached and can be lifted off, though this is not essential unless it is excessively thick. The back of the bud should still be in place.

A number of buds can be prepared at the same time provided that they are kept moist until they are wanted. To insert them, the earth is pulled away from the stock to expose the base of the stem, a T-shaped cut is made as low on the stem as possible and large enough to accommodate the bud, the bark is prised open and the bud slipped beneath it. It should be fastened into place. In nurseries a rubber tie is used, which also serves to keep the bud moist. A nurseryman may be willing to give or sell a few of these, and horticultural suppliers also sell them, though in much larger quantities than are likely to be wanted by a private gardener. Moist raffia or any other soft tying material can also be used. It should be positioned so that it grips the bark of the stock firmly over the scion but leaves the bud itself exposed. Rubber ties will fall off in due course; raffia or a more durable material may eventually need to be cut on the side opposite the bud to prevent constriction of the expanding stem.

If budding is successful, the union will be formed after about three weeks. When it is complete the leaf stalk will fall cleanly away. If a bud has failed there may be time to try again with another, as long as the bark will still lift easily.

Buds usually remain dormant until the spring, when they start into growth. Some of them grow in the year of budding, with the risk in higher latitudes that the shoot may not ripen and will thus be at risk from winter frosts. In the spring, just before growth starts, the stock should be pruned just above the bud. The top growth should not be removed earlier as the bud and stock unite much better when water and nutrients are passing between root and stem in the normal way.

CUTTINGS

Hardwood cuttings are easy for private gardeners to make. Many rose species and garden cultivars can be propagated by this method, though those with a large pith are much less likely to succeed. Selection of the stems is crucially important. They should be thoroughly ripened, firm and healthy. The soft upper growth and any remaining leaves should be removed, and the cutting made from the central portion. All the buds are retained. The cuttings should be 20 cm (8 in) to 30 cm (1 ft) long, made with a square cut at the bottom just below a bud, and a sloping one at the top just above a bud. The base can be dipped into rooting hormone of a strength suitable for hardwoods.

The cuttings can be put into the open ground, though a greater proportion will root if they are protected by a cold frame. In either case the method is the same. A trench is taken out with one side vertical, sharp sand is sprinkled along the base and the cuttings are then put in. They should be about 8 cm (3 in) apart, supported by the vertical face of the trench and pressed into the sand so that no air pockets are trapped beneath them. Two-thirds of the cutting should be underground. Fine soil is then put back and trodden down so that they are secure. After frost, which loosens the soil, they should be firmed again.

The cuttings can be made at any time that the stems are dormant. They should have rooted and be ready for spacing out in a nursery row a year later.

Plants grown on their own roots in this way produce shoots rather like suckers from below ground level, but these should not be removed.

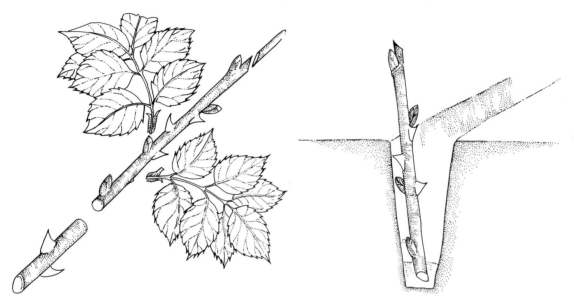

Taking cuttings of roses is a straightforward operation. Choose ripened healthy wood and remove any remaining leaves. Trim the bottom of the cutting square below a bud and the top above and slanting away from a bud. Insert the cutting in a small trench which has had some sharp sand placed in the bottom, then fill in with fine soil and firm down thoroughly

DIVISION

Roses grown on their own roots can produce shoots from below ground level, and once these are established they will generally form roots of their own. They can be separated from their parents during the dormant season using a sharp spade, and then planted in a nursery row to grow for a year. After planting the shoot should be pruned hard back to bring it into balance with its roots. Species that grow in clumps can be propagated particularly easily; they include *Rosa rugosa* and *R. pimpinellifolia* (*R. spinosissima*) together with their forms and hybrids. Most roses will occasionally oblige with a suitable stem. It is a matter of observing the habit of growth and reacting accordingly.

LAYERING

Layering is also comparatively easy for private gardeners. It involves bringing a stem into contact with the soil and pegging it there until roots form. It can only be done to roses with flexible stems that can be brought down to ground level, but this includes many shrub roses and ramblers.

The best time for layering is in the spring or in early and mid summer using young shoots. Older ones will not root easily, if at all. Firm, healthy growths must be chosen. A tongue can be made by making a short upward cut in the stem at the point where it is to be in contact with the ground. This should be 15 cm (6 in) to 30 cm (1 ft) back from the tip. The wound helps to stimulate root formation, though a right-angled bend constricts the flow of sap and will do the job just as well. In either case the stem should be pegged into the earth, staked upright, and covered by 8 cm (3 in) or more of soil. Roots will not form readily in dry soil, and if necessary the ground should be soaked afterwards. A brick or large stone should be placed over the soil to keep it cool and moist. If the job is done early, roots will have formed by the autumn and the shoot can be detached and grown on for a year before being put in a border. If the work is done late the layer should be left for another year. At pruning time the stems should be cut back so that top growth and roots are in balance with one another.

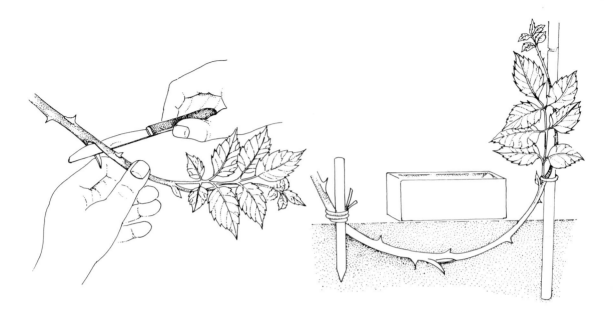

SEEDS

Growers wanting new cultivars use seed to produce them, though sometimes a shoot called a sport can arise spontaneously with sufficient differences to constitute a new kind, and this can be propagated vegetatively. Many stocks are also raised from seed.

Cultivars of roses have very involved pedigrees and will not reproduce themselves exactly by seed. Instead a bewildering range of different forms develops, most of them inferior to the parent. Species, on the other hand, do have the ability to grow from seed with little variation. There is one snag. The flowers are visited and fertilized by insects, which make no distinction between different kinds. In gardens several species and cultivars may be growing a short flight from one another, and this will almost certainly result in cross-pollination. Any seedlings that are grown will therefore be hybrids. To avoid this, hips should be taken from isolated bushes or from large plantations of a single kind, where the risk is smaller. The fruits should be picked as soon as they have coloured, because the production of substances like abscissic acid in the hip reinforces dormancy in the seed. The amount of seed in each hip varies considerably with the species. Some have only one or two while others, such as *Rosa rugosa*, can have as many as sixty.

On a small scale, seed can be sown at once and kept in cold frames. Some species, such as *Rosa moyesii*, germinate in the following spring, but even with these a proportion of the seed will need a second winter before it grows. Other species need two winters before germination takes place.

The seeds have an intrinsic dormancy, which has the effect in nature of deferring germination until a time of year when the young plant has the best chance of survival. It also spreads germination over more than one year, ensuring that one bad season does not wipe out all the progeny. Dormancy is broken by exposing the seeds to cool temperatures for a period. The process is called vernalization. This involves putting the hips into a container, each layer sandwiched between sand or any other medium that holds moisture, lets in air and is free from harmful substances. They are then put outside, perhaps against a north wall, and protected against rodents, which can steal the crop.

During the process the fruit rots, making it easier to extract the seeds. These are then sown in plant pots, boxes or any other container with plenty of drainage holes in the base, as they will not grow if waterlogged. Sandy compost is used. John Innes seed compost will do very well, as will soilless ones. Any light garden soil will also give good results. The seeds should be scattered thinly over the surface, and compost or sand sifted over the top so that they are just buried. The surface is then firmed and watered by steeping or by using a can with a fine rose.

The seeds are hardy, but to give the gardener better control the container can be put in a cold frame or cool greenhouse or onto the windowsill indoors. They do not need to be covered, but a sheet of glass placed over the top helps to speed the process of germination by reducing the rate at which the soil surface dries out. The glass needs to be wiped and turned every day to prevent droplets of condensation falling onto the soil, where they might cause damage to the germinating plant. The glass itself can be covered with a piece of newspaper to filter the light. It is removed at the first sign of germination.

Once the seeds have germinated and as soon as they are big enough to handle, the plants can be spaced out into boxes or pots. When they are large enough they can be put into bigger containers or planted in a row for a year, by which time they should have reached a size suitable for budding, in the case of stocks, or putting into the garden, in the case of species.

DAMPING OFF

All seedlings are prone to attacks by the soil fungi that cause damping off disease. Roses are no exception. The disease can cause young plants to rot even before they emerge from the soil, or later to rot at ground level, when the seedlings will fall over and die. Good cultivation is the best defence. The compost should be sterilized to kill off disease organisms. Most composts offered for sale will already have been treated or will be made of sterile materials. Pots and boxes should also be clean, and preferably disinfected before use. Any plants that develop symptoms should be got rid of at once. Greenhouses and frames should be kept clean and disinfected. High temperatures during germination encourage fungal activity. Chemical control can be obtained by drenching the soil with thiram before sowing.

MINIATURES

Miniature roses can be produced from softwood cuttings, taken in the spring from plants that have been forced. They require a mist propagation unit and are helped by the use of a hormone rooting compound. They can also be propagated by grafting in a warm greenhouse.

7
Pests and Diseases

CONTROLS WITHOUT CHEMICALS

Horticultural hypochondriacs will find plenty to engage their minds if they grow roses but it is easy to get the problem of pests and diseases out of porportion. In many gardens the plants can be grown successfully without recourse to chemical remedies of any kind.

Plant breeders have always paid attention to disease resistance, and most catalogues indicate whether a cultivar is immune or resistant to a particular disorder. There are enough good resistant sorts to furnish all but the largest gardens or the most comprehensive collections.

The choice of site and its preparation is another way to keep troubles in check. Roses do best in sunshine, where the stems can ripen in the autumn and where sturdy, healthy growth is encouraged. Good soil preparation, though not making the plants resistant to attack, is important in stimulating vigorous growth so that they can recover strongly afterwards.

Dead wood should be removed whenever it appears. Growths cut away during pruning should be removed and burned, and dead leaves should be raked from the rose beds, put on a bonfire or buried well out of the way. They can all act as centres from which disease spores or pests spread.

Weeds should also be removed. Some act as alternative hosts, and if they grow large enough they restrict air movement through the beds, increasing humidity and therefore the vulnerability of the bushes to some diseases.

Manual controls are also possible early in the life of an infestation. Caterpillars are easily seen and can be squashed by the stony hearted; a colony of aphids can be rubbed out of existence. Leaf rolling sawfly can be crushed, or the leaf it inhabits picked off and cremated. If only a few leaves are affected by black spot, they too can be removed and destroyed before the disease spreads. On a large scale these controls are impractical, but on a small one it is a useful means by which vigilant gardeners can keep some pests and diseases in check.

Not all pests are equally important. Some can be safely ignored by all but the gardener preparing flowers for an exhibit. An attack late in the growing season can also be disregarded, because although it may spoil the appearance of the plants it is not very likely to do them serious damage. Infestations that occur early in the year are generally a much more serious matter because the pest has time to increase in number throughout the growing season. Rust and black spot can cause the leaves to become unsightly and result in early leaf fall, sometimes by late July, if not controlled. The use of chemical sprays should be regarded as a last resort, even though modern research has developed highly effective ones.

CHEMICAL CONTROLS

Pest and disease killers can be applied in several forms. Liquid sprays are the most effective on roses, as they can penetrate into all the corners in which insects and

Opposite: The roses on the house echo those in the beds across a pleasant greensward

disease spores might lurk. They can be purchased as concentrates that are then diluted, or as powders or granules that must be dissolved in water before they can be used. They are usually already mixed with wetting agents to enable them to spread uniformly over leaves and stems, and with emulsifiers to allow the chemical to mix with water. They are best applied in the evening when the sun is off the foliage or sensitive varieties may be damaged. All parts of the plant should be treated, including the underside of the leaf and in some cases even the surface of the ground beneath the plants. When they have been mixed with water the sprays should be used at once because they soon lose their effectiveness.

Aerosol sprays can also be purchased, but although they are less troublesome they are very expensive, and because the chemical is more concentrated they need to be used with care to avoid scorching the flowers and leaves. They come into their own when trouble is just starting and only a limited area of the bush is affected, in which case a little first aid is all that is required and may prevent the pest or disease establishing itself and spreading further.

Dusts are also available for immediate use and are easy to apply. It is difficult to reach all parts of the plant with them, however, and they seldom settle evenly, so control may be incomplete and the treatment may need to be repeated.

Most garden chemicals have at least two names – one a name registered against a particular formulation, and sometimes several other proprietary names used by manufacturers to distinguish their own products. The insecticide dimethoate, for example, appears in more than thirty preparations with different brand names, not all of which include a reference to the active ingredient, though this will be declared somewhere on the outside of the container.

There are three main types of insecticide. Those that work only if you hit the insect with dust or spray are called contact insecticides, and include materials such as derris. An insect walking over the surface after it has been sprayed will also collect enough of the poison to kill it. Systemic insecticides are carried in the fluids of the plant, and kill all sap-sucking insects without injuring their predators or other beneficial creatures such as bees. Because they move inside the plant they do not need such a thorough coverage when applied. Dimethoate is a systemic insecticide in fairly common use against a number of pests, including aphids. Stomach poisons are used against pests like caterpillars, which eat the leaves of roses and will ingest the poison as well once the plants have been sprayed. Lindane, which is sold in more than fifty proprietary mixtures, is an example. Some chemicals act in more than one way, and several may be mixed together to control a number of pests and diseases at once.

SAFETY PRECAUTIONS

Garden chemicals need to be treated with caution. Safety precautions should always be scrupulously observed. They should be kept in their original containers, which should be clearly labelled and locked away out of the reach of children. Rubber gloves should be worn when handling a concentrate, whatever it is, and they should be washed after use. The maker's instructions should be followed exactly, especially as to dilution rates – the idea of using a spoonful for the pot is a good one only when making tea.

Spraying should only be done on a still day so the chemical does not drift onto plants that do not need it or onto you or other people. Not all the chemicals used on roses are enjoyed by other plants. Dimethoate, for example, can damage fuchsias, hydrangeas and some bedding plants, including begonias and asters, if it drifts onto them. The instructions will contain references to this, so they should be read with care. Chemicals should be kept out of watercourses and streams, and should not be tipped into drains that feed into them. Unused mixture can be disposed of by spraying it onto the ground beneath the bushes or by offering to spray a neighbour's roses, whose pests and diseases can easily become your own once they leap the fence. If either the dilute or the concentrate is accidentally splashed onto bare skin or, worse, gets in an eye it should be washed off at once using plenty of clean water. After use, equipment should be washed out thoroughly and empty bottles, tins or packets should be put in a sealed plastic bag in a dustbin and kept well out of the way of children and pets.

PESTS

Aphids
Several types of aphid or greenfly feed on roses, and all of them are a nuisance because they multiply so rapidly. They do damage by sucking the sap from developing stems, leaves and young buds, which become distorted or discoloured or even wither and die if the attack is very severe. They also excrete honeydew, which though not a nuisance in itself permits the growth of sooty moulds, and these make the plant unsightly and stop light from reaching the leaves. Anyone who has parked a car under a lime tree or a Norway maple in the early summer will know what a sticky mess the honeydew can make and how quickly the mould develops afterwards.

There is also an aphid that feeds on the roots. The first evidence of its presence is often the swarming activity of ants, which enjoy the honeydew. If the attack is extreme the plant will wilt. Sometimes the insects are visible at the base of the stem, though they are not always easy to pick out because they are brown and blend in well with their surroundings.

Several natural enemies feed on aphids, including birds and a variety of insects. Such a considerable food supply could hardly go untapped, but however assiduous they are, these creatures are unlikely to keep up with the population growth of a well-fed colony of greenfly, and chemical sprays are almost certain to be needed.

Liquid derris is an old remedy. It is sprayed over the whole bush, including all the cracks and crevices. It is effective, but a second spray a week later and possibly once after that will be needed because the chemical is not persistent, and any greenfly that were missed will have been capable of producing numerous offspring within a few days. Derris has the great merit for gardeners of not being poisonous, except to fish, though it will kill beneficial insects as well as pests. Pirimicarb kills aphids. Dimethoate, which is a systemic, is particularly useful against all sucking insects.

Capsids
Capsid bugs also have an occasional stab at roses, though they feed on a wide range of other plants as well. They cause distorted leaves and shoots, from which

they suck the sap when the growth is young and succulent. They can be controlled by systemic insecticides.

Caterpillars

The caterpillars of a number of different moths, though not of butterflies, have an appetite for roses, mostly for the leaves but also the buds and blossoms. A heavy infestation can do a great deal of mischief, though it does no permanent harm – apart, perhaps, from stunting growth.

The Lackey and Vapourer moth larvae and several others simply browse on the leaves and are comparatively easy to poison. Tortrix moth caterpillars roll the leaves and get protection inside them. They are harder to reach, though it is quite easy to pick the leaves by hand and destroy them.

The Tortrix caterpillars also burrow into flower buds, and those of the Tineid moths mine their way through the central tissues of the leaves. Because these pests attack other plants as well as roses, including several of economic significance, there is a wide range of chemical sprays for use against them. These include carbaryl, lindane, malathion, permethrin and pirimiphos-methyl. Derris and pyrethrum can also be used.

Large Flowered bush rose 'Peace' (see page 92) – perhaps most popular of them all

Shrub rose 'Fritz Nobis' (see page 109)

Chafers

The cockchafer, garden and rose chafer grubs feed voraciously on the roots of a wide range of plants. They are curved, plump grubs and will be familiar to many gardeners, especially those working on lighter soils and where there is woodland. They sometimes attack the roots of roses in gardens, but rarely to an extent that makes them worth controlling even if the symptoms of attack can be recognized.

The adult garden and rose chafers appear in late spring and early summer. The brown garden chafer is slightly smaller, up to 1 cm ($\frac{1}{2}$ in) long; the rose chafer is a bright yellowish green and rather pretty. The adults do more visible damage than their young, by attacking the flowers of roses, and as it is possible for a large swarm of beetles to appear the damage can sometimes be extensive.

During an attack it is possible to shake the stems over a container, in which case some of the beetles will fall in and can be killed. In preparing the ground for planting, especially if it was formerly under turf, the grubs may be found and can be destroyed. The gardener will be greatly assisted in this work by birds.

Spraying the flower buds with bromophos or diazinon will give some control, but it puts bees at risk.

Leaf hoppers

Attack by leaf hoppers causes a pale mottling of the foliage, and if the damage is extensive the leaves may fall before they should. This is a sucking insect, which punctures the tissue and feeds off the sap. Systemic insecticides give an effective control that is often incidental to killing colonies of aphids, which are usually seen first.

The frog hopper exudes cuckoospit, the frothy fluid that appears on a variety of plants in spring and summer. Because it is so easy to see it can be rubbed off and the insect inside squashed. Systemic insecticides used for other pests will control it. On its own it is hardly worth troubling about, though at its worst it can distort the growth of a young shoot.

Red spider mites

These are not often a serious pest of roses out of doors in temperate climates, but they are a problem in greenhouses, and in dry climates or seasons or in warm, sheltered places they can be a thorough nuisance. The mite is scarcely visible to the naked eye but the colonies soon become big ones when conditions are favourable, and they sometimes weave fine, silky webs. They suck the sap from the leaves, working from the underside, and cause points of discoloration that soon coagulate until eventually the whole leaf turns yellow and falls off. Dimethoate, malathion or fenitrothion will give control, but two or three applications will be needed.

Sawflies and slugworms

Sawflies and slugworms are both pests of roses and belong to the same group of insects. They both eat the leaves, but the symptoms of attack are rather different. The rose leaf rolling sawfly has the most dramatic effect. It lays its eggs in May or June by inserting them at the edge of the leaves, which react by rolling down and inwards, thus protecting the eggs and later the larvae as they develop. The damage is easy to see, and the leaves can be picked and destroyed. Sprays of pirimiphos-methyl during the egg-laying season can be made as a precaution.

Rose slugworm feeds on the top layer of the leaf, leaving the lower skin untouched. By the time it has finished eating the leaf looks like a grey, papery skeleton. It eats openly, so it can be killed by any of the chemicals used against caterpillars. Some other sawflies also feed on the open leaf and they can be killed in the same way.

The presence of the rose shoot borer sawfly can be recognized because individual shoots wilt without apparent reason. The grub lives on the pith, eating its way downwards through the middle of the shoot. Affected growths can be picked off and destroyed.

Thrips

Rose thrip is a tiny insect that is scarcely visible, but it breeds rapidly and its numbers build up dramatically. It is mainly a pest of greenhouse crops, but it will appear on roses out of doors in warmer climates or during hot summers in temperate areas. It causes the flowers to be misshapen and the leaves to become mottled and silvery in appearance. Systemic insecticides used for other pests will kill it, as will malathion and derris.

MINOR PESTS

Rose galls

Rose galls vary in appearance (one looks like a clump of fine moss) and are caused by gall wasps. They do little if any harm and can be ignored, though pernickety gardeners sometimes cut them off and burn them.

Rose hip fly
Another pest of little significance is the maggot of one of the fruit flies that attacks roses. It is not worth controlling, but may puzzle gardeners whose plants are attacked by it. The first signs are the speckles that discolour the outside of the hips where the flies puncture the skin to lay their eggs. Maggots later develop and eat the fruit, which then shrivels.

Scale insects
European brown scale, peach scale and scurfy scale all attack roses and cluster on the bark. They are sap-sucking pests, and so are controlled incidentally by systemic insecticides used against more obvious and troublesome insects. On roses they are rarely more than a source of minor unsightliness.

Leaf cutting bee
The leaf cutting bee cuts semicircular pieces out of the edge of the leaves. It rarely does enough damage to make control worthwhile.

Animal pests
Some people find that their roses are eaten by red deer in spring, and perhaps also by roe deer in summer. There is no remedy that is acceptable. High fencing will

Some common rose troubles: (from left to right, top to bottom) frog hopper – cuckoo spit – (see page 79), leaf-rolling sawfly damage, leaf-cutter bee damage, black spot (see page 82), failure to open (see page 85)

keep deer out but is unsightly and very expensive. Vigorous cultivars and plenty of manure will enable the plants to recover from an occasional attack.

Rabbits and hares will also eat roses, some cultivars seeming to be more attractive to them than others. The young stems and leaves of 'Super Star' and 'Pink Parfait', for example, seem to be particularly popular. In some areas there are rabbit protection societies or individual trappers who can be employed to keep rabbits under control, though the problem is one of a whole district not of an individual garden. It is feasible to fence rosebeds to keep rabbits out, or the young shoots can be sprayed with a chemical deterrent.

Diseases

Mildew, black spot and rust are the three diseases that cause most trouble on roses, though in some countries virus diseases are also a major problem.

Black spot

Black spot attacks the foliage, and is first visible as round, black or dark purple blotches with uneven edges. It can cause the leaves to turn yellow and fall early and also weakens the plants, which makes them more vulnerable to damage in severe winter weather in higher latitudes. The main offence is a visual one, because the disease makes the plants look very unsightly and woebegone.

Resistant cultivars should be chosen where possible; fallen leaves should be raked up and burned or buried well away from the plants. If previous experience suggests that an attack is likely to occur, preventative sprays should be used to forestall it, because once infection has taken place the fungus cannot be eradicated and the infected leaves will continue to harbour the disease and develop its symptoms, though its spread to newly developing foliage can be prevented.

Spraying with captan, maneb or mancozeb should be done after pruning to ensure that spores resting on the plant are killed. The soil surface should also be sprayed to kill any that are there. In areas where the disease is common, or if susceptible cultivars are involved, regular further sprayings, beginning in late spring or early summer, will be necessary to protect newly developing leaves. The spray should be applied to both the top and the underside of the foliage, and to the developing shoots.

Mildew

Powdery mildew is very common. It appears as a dusty white growth on both leaves and stems. It is conspicuous and makes the plants unsightly, though it is superficial and does little lasting harm.

Good hygiene gives some control. Prunings and fallen leaves should be burned. Climbers and ramblers growing against a wall, where the roots may get dry, are very prone to attack. Preparing the ground thoroughly before planting with plenty of organic matter, and annual mulching to retain water, helps to reduce susceptibility. Some cultivars are resistant and these should be preferred, though none are immune. Spraying will control the disease, and because it is common on a wide range of plants some of which are commercially important, a number of materials is available. They include benomyl, bupirimate, dinocap and several others.

Opposite: *Rosa rugosa* 'Alba' (see page 113)

Rust

Rust is a difficult problem in some areas and can cause defoliation, which will kill a plant if it suffers a series of annual attacks. In spring the fungus appears on the young shoots, which may be distorted. It can be seen as an orange-coloured dust. In summer it attacks the leaves, which show yellow blotches on the surface. The fungus itself can be seen on the underside as pale orange or black spots, depending on the stage of the fungus. In severe attacks the plants may lose all their foliage by the end of July, and then look gaunt and unlovely through what should be their season of glory. Control can be obtained by spraying with mancozeb, maneb and other chemicals. In areas where the disease is prevalent regular applications are necessary.

Virus

In some countries virus diseases spread slowly in roses and do not kill the bushes, though they weaken them and make the foliage unsightly. Buying plants from a reputable nursery that has taken care to use only healthy propagating material is one of the best securities against the infection. The symptoms depend on the virus concerned, but they include various patterns of yellow or pale green foliar discoloration: one appears along the veins, one as a yellow mosaic, a third as ringspots, and another looks like the outline of an oak leaf.

In some countries virus is a serious problem, and other forms occur. For example, in Australia rose wilt is capable of killing a plant. The virus is transmitted by sap-sucking insects as well as by the use of infected material in propagation. Early symptoms include defoliation of the young stems, starting at the top, after which they die back. Eventually the whole bush is killed.

Other diseases

A number of disorders, some of which can attack any garden shrub, can also be troublesome to roses. **Honey fungus** occasionally gets into a rose bed and kills the bushes. It attacks the roots first and progresses until it rings the base of the stem beneath the bark as a white plate of fungal mycelium. By then the plant will be lost. Affected bushes should be removed, along with the soil around them, and burned.

Grey mould or botrytis (the name also describes the appearance of the fungus) attacks a variety of garden plants and can kill off weak and unripened wood. It is one of the common causes of die back following frost damage or faulty pruning. The disease can be kept in check by allowing air to circulate freely among the roses. This is achieved by keeping down weeds, by pruning to avoid a clutter of crowded stems, and by removing and destroying dead wood. Pruning should be done in the spring, when healing is likely to be most rapid, using sharp secateurs with the cuts correctly placed. The chemical chlorothalonil will control it if necessary.

In some climates and in greenhouses **downy mildew** causes pale grey or purplish spotting of the leaves and will result in premature leaf fall. Zineb gives control.

Three kinds of fungus causing cankers can attack the stems of roses, which are then distorted and wrinkled in appearance and may die back. **Brown canker** can be a serious disease in the United States, and has been recorded in Britain and

Europe. Large brown cankers grow on the stems, which often die. Infected wood should be cut out and burned.

Rose leaf spot is caused by a fungal parasite. The young spots are purplish, turning brown as they get older. They become about 5 mm ($\frac{1}{4}$ in) across. Gardeners sometimes confuse this with black spot.

Crown gall, which is a bacterial disease, can attack roses as it does many other plants. The galls vary in size and appear both on stems and roots near ground level. *R. manettii* stocks are sometimes victims. It is controlled by growing the plants on clean land, which is normal in rose nurseries because of the need to avoid soil sickness. The disease does no real harm but it does cause enquiries from time to time, and the galls are ugly.

OTHER DISORDERS

Failure to open
Sometimes, particularly in wet weather, flowers fail to open and remain as rather sorry-looking, decaying balls. The outer petals appear to decay and meld together into a corset that stops the flower expanding. Some cultivars are more susceptible than others, and the condition varies with the location and the season. There is no cure. If a cultivar is a persistent offender year after year it should be removed and replaced with something better.

Hormone weedkillers
Selective weedkillers based on hormones are in common use in gardens to kill broad-leaved weeds growing in lawns. They cause twisting, distorted growth on the young shoots of roses and can kill the plants. The weedkiller can drift onto them if it is used when there is a breeze, or it might be splashed on by careless application. Even the fumes can cause damage if the weedkiller is used on still, humid days when the vapour remains in the vicinity of the bushes. Grass cuttings from lawns that have been treated with weedkiller may still contain enough of the substances to cause damage when used as a mulch.

Mineral deficiency
Too much lime in the soil can lock up some essential elements and make life difficult for roses. Iron is one example. It is essential for growth and the production of healthy green leaves. You can see its effect by treating turf with lawn sand, which contains sulphate of iron. Its application produces a vivid, rich verdure. If the plant cannot extract iron from the soil the opposite occurs and the leaves become sickly and yellow. In the case of roses the effect is first seen as a yellow band around the edge of the leaf and along its veins. Eventually the whole leaf turns yellow and falls off. To restore health iron can be sprayed onto roses, but it must be in the form of a compound that is soluble and capable of being absorbed by the foliage. Several manufacturers market suitable brands. Repeated applications throughout the growing season may be needed.

A to Z
of
Roses

A prolific display of flowers from 'Madame Grégoire Staechelin'

Classifying roses is a technical matter, but as this guide is intended for gardeners in general rather than for expert rosarians in particular I have gathered the species and cultivars in the following pages into the groups in which they generally appear in catalogues. For this reason I have elected to use the term patio roses for one of the groups even though it does not form part of the approved system of nomenclacture. It also seems a useful classification for ordinary garden purposes and so is likely to hold its currency. Similarly, I have not sought to subdivide shrub roses into groups related to their origin nor to separate the species from the rest. Gardeners will generally find a place for them on the basis of their colour, scent and characteristics of growth rather than their parentage. Each group is then subdivided into colour ranges, though these can give only an approximate guide as, for example, the term 'red' embraces many different shades. I have chosen to use this approach because when planning a rose border, or looking for new plants to introduce into an existing one, colour is one of the first considerations. The most frequent gardening enquiry that I deal with goes like this: 'I am looking for a red rose for my garden. Can you tell me the name of a good variety?' Once the name has been given the next question is, 'Does it have a scent?' I hope the arrangement that follows will permit these and similar questions to be answered.

Many cultivars blossom during two main periods a few weeks apart, when the plants are at their showiest. Because some flowers are present right through the season, not only during the main flushes, I have used the term 'flowers throughout the season' to describe them. The word remontant, which means blooming more than once in the same season, is often used to describe this phenomenon.

Bush roses

The once clear division between Hybrid Tea and Floribunda roses has now almost disappeared, and the terms have been replaced. Most, though not all, catalogues now list bush roses under the new headings of Large Flowered and Cluster Flowered roses, and this arrangement is also followed here.

Bush roses are also sometimes called bedding roses, which is a reflection of their main use in formal flowerbeds. They are well adapted for this purpose because they provide a mass of colour over a long season, but they can be used in other ways as well: in groups, as specimens, as hedges, or incorporated into borders of other plants to provide colour at times when many shrubs are dull. Some are useful for cut flowers.

Nurserymen have recently introduced another category, which they call patio roses. These are dwarf kinds that are valuable for small gardens, for use as edgings, and for containers. Because they have a distinct use they have been considered separately in the lists that follow.

Roses vary in height according to the cultivar, but they also respond to the conditions in which they are grown. It is thus impossible to be precise about heights. The word 'short' is used in the following pages to denote a plant that may grow to a height of 75 cm (2½ ft), 'medium' for those up to 1.2 m (4 ft), and 'tall' for those that can exceed this height.

All the cultivars start to flower about mid summer – earlier in lower latitudes, later in the higher ones. Bred to flower more or less continuously until winter intervenes, depending on the climate the main displays occur in two or three periods, when many buds open together.

Rose cultivars sometimes appear under different names in different countries. For example, 'Super Star' is also known as 'Tropicana', 'Peace' as 'Gioia', 'Gloria Dei' or as 'Mme A. Meilland', 'Iceberg' as 'Schneewittchen' or 'Feé des Neiges', and so on. The names below are those in use in the United Kingdom. The American Rose Society is the International Registration Authority for roses, and publishes a checklist called *Modern Roses*. It describes all the present cultivars, giving details of the flower, foliage, where possible the name of the parents, and the breeder, so the rose can be accurately identified. It also lists any synonyms. Breeders naming a new rose should check the list to ensure that the same name is not already in use for a different plant. Some catalogues now also list the code name of a cultivar – that is, the name the breeder uses first until its popular name is chosen, usually for commercial considerations or perhaps to honour an individual or organization. Thus the Cluster Flowered rose 'Volunteer' was known as 'Harquaker' until it was named in honour of Voluntary Service Overseas, and 'International Herald Tribune' was first known as 'Harquantum'. It allows even greater certainty in identifying roses across national and linguistic boundaries.

Apart from the question of synonyms, climatic conditions affect the popularity of cultivars. A different range is grown, for example, in warmer countries from that in cooler ones; thus 'Alec's Red', though bred in the north of Scotland, does best in hotter summers further south, while 'Piccadilly' does well in the north but the flower fades badly when exposed to the more intense sunshine of lower latitudes.

LARGE FLOWERED BUSH ROSES

MULTICOLOURED

'Gay Gordons' Red and yellow. Short. It is still grown for its mixture of colours, but it suffers from disease and needs regular spraying.

'Harry Wheatcroft' Red striped with yellow. Medium height. Needs regular spraying to keep black spot in check.

'Piccadilly' Red and yellow. Medium height. Prone to black spot. It fades quickly in hot, very sunny climates or seasons, but its unusual colour keeps it in cultivation.

'Rose Gaujard' Deep pink with a white reverse and base. Medium to tall. The flowers are shapely and large, the bushes disease-resistant; it sits uneasily in a mixed planting and should be kept on its own.

PINK SHADES

'Abbeyfield Rose' Deep pink. Short to medium height. The pretty flower and compact growth make this a particularly good rose to use in a bed. Disease resistant.

'Blessings' Salmon pink. Medium height, with plentiful flowers.

'Chicago Peace' Pink with yellow at the base of the petal. Slight scent. Tall. This is a sport from the famous cultivar 'Peace'. It has very large flowers, makes a good cut flower and can be grown as a shrub. It is suitable for bedding only in a large space, and even then can look ungainly, but it will make a strong hedge.

'Fyvie Castle' Pink and apricot. Short. Attractive, healthy foliage.

'Keepsake' Cherry pink. Tall. Scented flowers and disease-resistant foliage.

'Lovely Lady' Rose pink. Short to medium height. Scented and disease resistant.

'Margaret Thatcher' Pretty, pale pink. Medium height. The flower is long lasting and is good for cut flowers.

'Mischief' Salmon pink. Medium height. Slightly scented, with large and attractive flowers, but this cultivar is sometimes prone to disease.

'Neville Gibson' Pink. Medium height. The flowers are very large and are suitable for exhibiting.

'Chicago Peace'
(see page 89)

'Paul Shirville' Salmon pink. Medium height. The flowers are very pretty, scented, and attractive for cutting.

'Pink Favorite' Bright pink. Medium height. Its large flowers and their attractive shape make it a good rose for showing. Little scent. Its glossy, healthy, bright green leaves show the flowers to advantage.

'Prima Ballerina' Deep pink. Medium to tall. Vulnerable to mildew and other diseases and needs regular spraying, but its perfume and large, pretty flowers have kept it in catalogues.

'Rebecca Claire' Pale pink with a shade of orange. Medium height. The sweet perfume of this rose makes it well worth a place in the garden.

'Silver Jubilee' Salmon pink with a blending of other tints. Medium height. Slight scent. The foliage is pretty in spring and resists diseases. This rose is almost ideal for bedding, with abundant, enduring leaves and plentiful flowers with an attractive shape.

'Sweetheart' Deep pink. Medium height. The flowers, sweetly scented, last well in water. It is a good exhibitors' rose.

'Polar Star' (see page 92)

RED AND ORANGE SHADES

'Alec's Red' Dark cherry red. Medium height. Strongly scented. The flowers are good for cutting, and their sweet scent can pervade a room. The foliage is disease resistant.

'Alexander' Very bright vermilion red. Tall, upright growth. Slight scent. It has a sport called 'L'Oreal Trophy', which is pale orange and has the same habit of growth, so they can be planted together. They are both good for cut flowers and also make strong hedges.

'Can Can' Orange-red. Short. Large flowers that are sweetly scented.

'Cheshire Life' Vermilion red. Medium height. Slightly scented.

'Corso' Orange. Medium height. Slightly scented. Good for cut flowers and the blooms last well in water.

'Doctor Dick' Orange. Medium height. Sweetly scented. The attractive shape of the flower makes it good for exhibiting.

'Doris Tysterman' Bright orange-red. Medium height. Scented. This cultivar is prone to mildew, and if it is chosen regular precautionary sprays are advised.

'Ernest H. Morse' Dark red. Medium height, but can get taller in some conditions. Scented. Healthy, dark green foliage.

'Forgotten Dreams' Deep red. Medium height. Sweetly scented.

'Fragrant Cloud' Coral red. Medium height. Sweetly scented. Its perfume is its principal merit, and makes it a good rose for cutting. It is also used by exhibitors. Protection against unsightly black spot is advisable.

'Innoxa Femille' Deep, dark red. Slightly scented. Medium height. Its thorny stems make it suitable as a low-growing hedge.

'Ingrid Bergman' Dark red, large, handsome flowers. Tall. Can be used as a shrub, a specimen, as a bedding rose or to make a hedge.

'Josephine Bruce' Very dark red. Medium height. Large, scented blooms. This is an older cultivar, and needs regular attention to keep it free from mildew, but its dark, shapely flowers with a hint of black in the colour can be very beautiful.

'Lovers Meeting' Orange. Short, as its name implies! The flowers have an attractive shape, which makes them useful for cutting, and also contrast well with the bronze foliage.

'Loving Memory' Bright crimson flowers. Tall, rather stiff habit of growth. Slightly scented. The name, and perhaps also the colour, make it popular for commemorative planting.

'National Trust' Deep crimson. Short. It has strong, healthy leaves, which are pretty in spring when their coppery colour shows to advantage. It flowers freely and enjoys good health.

'Precious Platinum' Bright red, large flowers. Medium height. It makes a good cut flower.

'Red Devil' Scarlet. Medium height. Scented. The reason for growing this cultivar is the size of its flowers, though this does make them vulnerable to damage in bad weather. It is impressive in an exhibit.

'Royal William' Crimson, velvety flowers. Medium height. Sweetly scented. Healthy, dark green leaves.

'Super Star' Vermilion. Tall. A scented cultivar that is prone to mildew and needs regular spraying to keep it clean. Its brilliantly coloured flowers, which are freely produced, have sustained its popularity.

'Troika' Orange-red with a darker centre. Tall. Healthy, bright green leaves.

'Wendy Cussons' Rosy red. Medium to tall. Sweetly scented. Makes a good cut flower, and because of its attractive shape is also a good exhibition rose. It may suffer from black spot in some seasons.

'Pot o' Gold' (see page 92)

'Iced Ginger' (see page 96)

WHITE

'Beryl Bach' White with a yellow tint in the petals, which are flushed with crimson towards the edges. Medium height. Sweetly scented. The flower is an unusual shade that is interesting in the garden and is attractive as a cut flower.

'Elizabeth Harkness' Creamy flowers shaded with pink. Medium height. Sweetly scented. The flowers are large and attractive for cutting.

'Pascali' White with a creamy tint. Medium height. The flowers are good for cutting, and the upright growth makes the plant useful as a hedge.

'Polar Star' White shaded with cream. Tall. The foliage is dark and healthy, and sets off the flowers attractively.

'Polly' Cream with a darker shade within. Short. The sweetly scented flower has a beautiful shape, which has kept it in catalogues for more than sixty years.

'Pristine' White with a shade of pink. Medium height. Sweetly scented.

YELLOW AND APRICOT SHADES

'Dutch Gold' Golden yellow. Medium height. Large, scented flowers.

'Freedom' Deep yellow. Short. Healthy foliage.

'Gold Star' Yellow. Medium height. The flowers are comparatively small, but are carried on strong stems that are good for cut flowers.

'Grandpa Dickson' Lemon yellow, shaded with pink. Medium height. Slightly scented. The flowers are large, and good for showing.

'Julia's Rose' Copper coloured with some pink. Medium height. The flower is unusual in its colour, and this makes it interesting for flower arranging. The bush itself is not very attractive.

'Just Joey' Copper coloured. Medium height. Slightly scented. The flowers are good for use in an arrangement.

'King's Ransom' Deep yellow. Medium height. Slightly scented. The blooms are large and make good cut flowers.

'L'Oreal Trophy' Pale salmon colour. Tall. This sport of 'Alexander' shares its considerable vigour. It can be used for cut flowers and is attractive in bud.

'Peace' Pale yellow flushed with pink. Tall. This is one of the famous roses that has remained prominent in catalogues for more than forty years. Its flowers are very large and can be used for cutting. It is large and robust enough to form a shrub, and can be used as a successful hedge. Generally resistant to disease, and vigorous enough to brush off an occasional attack of black spot.

'Peaudouce' Primrose yellow. Medium height. Its bushy habit makes the plant attractive for bedding, and its pleasant colour makes it a good cut flower as well.

'Peer Gynt' Rich yellow, slightly shaded with pink as the flowers get older. Slightly scented. Medium height.

'Pot o' Gold' Clear yellow. Medium height. Slightly scented.

'Rosemary Harkness' Yellow and salmon shades in a pretty mélange. Medium height. Scented.

'Simba' Clear yellow. Medium height. The flowers have an attractive shape.

'Sunset Song' Yellow with shades of copper. Medium height. The colour is unusual, and this makes it worth growing either for bedding or for cut flowers.

'Sutter's Gold' Yellow with shades of pink. Very fragrant. Medium height. Its scent and long, pretty buds justify its place, though the bush is seldom well clothed in leaves.

'Whisky Mac' Deep yellow shaded with amber. Medium height. Sweetly scented. This cultivar, although worth growing for its scent, is prone to disease and needs regular spraying to prevent attack. It is also inclined to suffer cold damage in cooler climates.

OTHER COLOURS

'Blue Moon' Lilac, not blue. Medium height. Scented. This cultivar is worth growing as a novelty or for cut flowers.

CLUSTER FLOWERED BUSH ROSES

PINK SHADES

'Anisley Dickson' Salmon pink. Medium height. The shapely, attractive flowers are freely produced.

'Busy Lizzie' Rose pink. Short. The buds are a pretty, pointed shape and the bushes are neat and compact.

'Congratulations' Rose pink. Tall. The plant gets too big for small spaces: it makes a showy 1.2 m (4 ft) high hedge. The flowers are good for cutting.

'Dearest' Rose pink. Short to medium height. Scented. It is pretty in a flowerbed, but it is susceptible to black spot and also to rust, and in wet weather the flowers are soon spoilt. In spite of this it is still widely grown.

'Deb's Delight' Salmon, pink centred. Short. The buds are particularly pretty.

'Elizabeth of Glamis' Salmon pink. Medium height. Scented. Though still widely grown it only does well on fertile, well-drained soils. Vulnerable to disease, needs regular spraying. The flowers are pretty when open, but there are now better cultivars in the same colour range.

'Escapade' Rosy red, white in the centre. Medium to tall. Scented. This is a very pretty, open rose showing its relationship with the wild hedgerow flowers. It has a boss of golden stamens which are conspicuous in the centre. It can be used for bedding, or it fits prettily into a border of other plants.

'Fragrant Delight' Salmon orange. Medium to tall. Sweetly scented. This is a pretty, showy rose suitable for bedding and, because of its upright growth, for a hedge. It grows strongly; disease resistant.

'Inner Wheel' Pale pink, darkening towards the base of the petals. Short. The flowers are dainty, with an unusual colour. Disease resistant.

'Laughter Lines' Rose pink, with shadings of red and gold. Short to medium height. Cheerful open flowers. Would look good in a border. Disease resistant.

'Our Hilda' Deep pink. Medium height. Attractive flowers in the bud. Disease resistant.

'Pink Parfait' Pink, with cream at the base of the petal. Medium height. Slightly scented. The flower is attractive in the bud and resists disease.

'Queen Elizabeth' Light pink. Tall. This can become a very large shrub indeed and is not suitable for a small garden. It can be used as a hedge, planted as a specimen, or used in a shrub border. It is not a good rose for a flowerbed, where it really grows too tall and out of step with its neighbours.

'Radox Bouquet' Rose pink. Medium to tall. Sweetly scented. The flowers open into a pleasing traditional, old-fashioned shape.

'Sea Pearl' Salmon pink, shaded with peach. Tall. Scented. The plant resists disease. Because of its height it is not very suitable for a flowerbed but can be planted as a small group in a border, where the blend of colours in the flower shows to advantage.

'Sexy Rexy' Rose pink. Medium height. The name suggests a more macho colour than the rose possesses, but it is pretty.

'Shona' Coral pink. Small to medium height. The pretty flowers are produced in large trusses.

'Wandering Minstrel' Salmon pink, tinted with orange. Medium height. The flower is pretty both in bud and when open. It is disease resistant.

'Wishing' Pink. Short. The flowers are a clear, rich colour, and the buds attractive and produced in considerable numbers. Disease resistant.

'Eye Paint'

RED AND ORANGE SHADES

'Anne Cocker' Vermilion. Medium height. The flowers are comparatively small, but when cut they have great powers of endurance. If they are steeped up to the neck in water for 24 hours before they are used to make an arrangement they will stay fresh for a fortnight.

'Avocet' Orange, darker in the bud and paling as it gets older. Medium height. The colour is as elusive as the bird.

'Beautiful Britain' Light, clear red. Medium height. Can also be used to make a hedge.

'Bonfire Night' Orange-scarlet with yellow. Medium height.

'Brown Velvet' Red with an orange-brown shade. Medium height. Too sombre for use in a large flowerbed, but interesting for arrangements.

'City of Bradford' Bright red and orange. Medium height. The colour is strong and makes a showy splash of colour.

'Disco Dancer' Bright, glowing orange-red. Medium height. Disease resistant. It can be used as a hedge for a colour shock.

'Evelyn Fison' Rich red. Medium height. This is an old cultivar, but it remains popular because of the intense colour of the flowers.

'Iceberg'

'Eye Paint' Scarlet with a white centre. Tall. The single flowers have a showy boss of golden stamens at the centre. Is vigorous enough to be used as a shrub.

'Geraldine' Orange. Medium height. A good plant where a bold, dashing colour is required as a focal point in a garden.

'Intrigue' Very dark red. Short. Its distinctive colour can seem almost black.

'Invincible' Rich red. Medium height. Like all floribundas this rose appears to advantage in a flowerbed; upright growth, so it can be used to make a hedge, though the name exaggerates its impregnability.

'Lilli Marlene' Bright, velvet red. Medium height. This is also an older cultivar, which has survived because of the strong colour and abundance of the flowers.

'Lively Lady' Bright vermilion. Medium height. Slight scent.

'Matangi' Orange-red with a white shading at the petal edge. Medium height. Scented.

'Memento' Salmon vermilion. Medium height. Very large clusters of slightly scented flowers. Disease resistant.

'Olive' Rich, clear red. The flowers are large and verge on luminosity. Medium to tall. Healthy, dark green leaves.

'Champagne Cocktail' (see page 96)

'**Rob Roy**' Dark, rich red. Tall. The attractive shape of the flowers makes this worth growing. Disease resistant.

'**Sue Ryder**' Salmon orange. Medium height. The colour varies, depending on the age of the flowers.

'**The Times**' Crimson red. Medium height. Disease resistant.

'**Trumpeter**' Bright vermilion red. Short. Suitable for the front of a border or a small bed near a path. Disease resistant.

WHITE SHADES

'**Iceberg**' White, the buds tinged with pink. Medium to tall. Little scent. This is a very fine rose that forms a graceful shrub if pruned lightly. It is prone to black spot.

'**Len Turner**' Creamy white, flushed pink. Short to medium height.

'**Margaret Merril**' White with a hint of pale pink in the colour. Medium height.

The flower is very pretty in both colour and shape. May need protection against disease.

YELLOW AND APRICOT SHADES

'**Allgold**' Clear yellow. Short. Slight scent. Now more than 30 years old, this rose is still widely grown. It is not very vigorous and needs good conditions to do well.

'**Amber Queen**' Amber yellow. Short. Scented. The pretty flowers show to advantage against the dark, shiny foliage. Disease resistant.

'**Anne Harkness**' Apricot yellow. Medium to tall. This is a very fine rose recommended for all garden purposes. Its first show of flowers comes a little later than most cultivars.

'**Arcadian**' Apricot yellow. Medium height. The flowers have a pretty shape, with a colour range from pink to gold.

'Arthur Bell' Golden yellow. Medium to tall. Sweetly scented flowers fade as they get older. Disease resistant.

'Bright Smile' Yellow. Short. A good, clear colour that offers a bright focus for the front of a border or for a small bed. Disease resistant.

'Burma Star' Amber yellow. Tall. Slightly scented.

'Conqueror's Gold' Yellow flushed with pink. Short. The flowers are very eye-catching and handsome, and would make a brave show in a border or a bed.

'Glenfiddich' Golden amber. Medium height. Scented. The dark foliage provides an attractive setting for the flowers. Disease resistant. The plant does well in higher latitudes, but is not so much esteemed in lower ones.

'Honeymoon' Yellow. Medium to tall. Slightly scented. This vigorous plant does well in higher latitudes, but in lower ones petals bleach quickly and flowering is sometimes disappointing.

'Iced Ginger' The colour is a blend of buff, ivory and pink. Medium to tall. Disease resistant. The plant is attractive for cut flowers because of its unusual, pretty blend of colours. Its habit of growth is unattractive, and in some locations this can be a disadvantage.

'Judy Garland' Deep yellow. Medium height. As the flowers become older the petals develop a pretty orange-red rim.

'Korresia' Bright yellow. Small to medium. Scented. Disease resistant. The flowers keep their colour well as they age.

'Mountbatten' Clear yellow. Medium to tall. As well as being attractive in a flowerbed, where the healthy leaves set off the yellow flowers, it is large and vigorous enough to make a shrub or a hedge.

'Penelope Keith' Bright yellow. Short. The flowers are small but pretty.

'Princess Alice' Yellow. Medium height. Disease resistant. The large trusses and the clear colour of the flower make this an attractive cultivar.

'Southampton' Apricot, flushed with pink. Medium to tall. Is suitable for a hedge or will fit into a shrub border. However, it is too large to look at ease in a small bed.

OTHER SHADES

'Champagne Cocktail' Yellow flecked with red. Medium height. Scented.

'Dame of Sark' Orange-red, with yellow reverse and base. Medium to tall. The colour is striking though the flowers are not individually handsome. Disease resistant.

'Festival Fanfare' Pale orange with white stripes. Tall. Because of its height it is not a very suitable plant for a flowerbed, but it could find a place in a border.

'Greensleeves' Greenish shade. Medium height. The colour is novel rather than beautiful, but it may well attract flower arrangers.

'Hannah Gordon' White with a rich pink fringe to the petal. Medium height.

'Masquerade' Bright yellow and pink. The flowers become increasingly red as they get older.

'Sheila's Perfume' Yellow with a red fringe to the petals. Medium height. Scented. The colour is a cheerful one and makes a bright contribution to a garden. It is an example of a rose raised by an amateur breeder.

'Shocking Blue' Not really blue, of course, but lilac with mauve. Medium height. Scented. The colour is difficult to fit into a garden but the cut flowers are of interest.

'Vital Spark' Yellow flushed with red. Medium height.

Climbers, scramblers and ramblers

This group of plants has been very much improved in the last two or three decades, especially by the introduction of cultivars that flower more or less continuously through the summer months. A few older kinds with particular qualities survive in catalogues, for example 'Mermaid', which was bred in the early years of this century and is still esteemed for its large, single flowers, or 'Albertine', which flowers briefly in early summer but with such exuberance that it is still valued. Some of the climbing cultivars, such as 'Maigold' and 'Golden Showers', make attractive shrubs and can be used for specimen planting. Many are suitable for propagating as weeping standards.

The following is a selection from the cultivars that are currently available. They are grouped according to the colour of their flowers, though it should be said by way of warning that the term red, for example, encompasses a wide range of associated shades.

Roses vary in dimension depending on how and where they are grown, and it is not possible to be precise about their eventual heights. The figures given are therefore only approximations.

MULTICOLOURED

'Handel' Creamy white, semi-double flowers edged with red with an elusive (i.e. faint) scent. It flowers prettily throughout the summer. Height 3.5 m (11 ft). Can be used as a shrub.

'Joseph's Coat' Yellow-orange and red semi-double flowers produced throughout the summer. Height 2.5 m (8 ft). It can also be used as a pillar or grown as a shrub.

PINK SHADES

'Aloha' Pink double flowers shaded with salmon in the bud, flowering throughout the summer. It is not a very vigorous climber but can reach 2.1 m (7 ft). The plant can also be left unpruned to make an attractive arching shrub, in which form it is also suitable for specimen planting.

'Bantry Bay' Light pink, semi-double flowers produced throughout the summer, abundant mid-green leaves. Height 3.5 m (11 ft).

'Compassion' Salmon pink flowers, with a shading of orange, appearing throughout the summer and very sweetly scented. The leaves are dark green and provide a good foil for the flowers. Height 3 m (10 ft), but it can also be grown as an arching shrub for use as a specimen or in a border. It is, however, one of the very best climbing roses, with an abundance of flowers.

'Madame Grégoire Staechelin' Large, deep pink, double flowers splashed with crimson. It only flowers once, in early summer, but is magnificent in full bloom. The foliage is glossy and dark green. It grows to 4.5 m (15 ft).

'Malaga' Deep pink, double flowers produced throughout the summer, with a light fragrance. Glossy, dark green leaves. Height 2.5 m (8 ft).

'Morning Jewel' Bright pink, scented flowers throughout the summer, though the first blooming is the best one. It enjoys good health. Height 2.5 m (8 ft).

'Pink Perpetue' Pink double flowers with a darker reverse, in large clusters that reappear in early autumn. Height 2.5 m (8 ft).

'New Dawn' Shell pink, double flowers produced throughout the summer. The glossy leaves are rather small but abundant. Height 3.5 m (11 ft). It can be grown on pillars or arches, or will grow through a hedge or another shrub. It will make a large, arching, rather spreading hedge.

Thornless climbing rose 'Zéphirine Drouhin'

'Summer Wine' Pretty, coral pink single flowers with a sweet perfume, produced throughout the summer. Height 3 m (10 ft).

'Zéphirine Drouhin' Deep pink, semi-double flowers, sweetly scented and flowering throughout the summer. Matt, pale green leaves tinted with crimson. This cultivar is subject to mildew and black spot; its particular interest is that it is virtually free from thorns, and this has kept it in catalogues for more than a century. It will grow to 3.5 m (11 ft), and can also be used as a shrub.

RED AND ORANGE SHADES

'Alec's Red, Climbing' Large, deep red, double flowers throughout the summer. Very fragrant. It is not very vigorous as a climber, and struggles to reach 2.1 m (7 ft) in height.

'Altissimo' Large, bright red single flowers that reappear during the summer. It has handsome, healthy dark green leaves. Height 4.5 m (15 ft).

'Morning Jewel' (see page 97)

'Copenhagen' Large, bright red, scented double flowers throughout the summer months. The foliage is healthy and coppery in colour. Height 4.5 m (15 ft).

'Danse des Sylphes' Bright red flowers in clusters. The flowers are produced throughout the summer and have a faint perfume. Height 3.7 m (12 ft).

'Danse du Feu' Bright orange-red, semi-double flowers, freely produced in clusters throughout the summer months but starting early. Dark green, glossy leaves. Height 3 m (10 ft). It has the advantage of tolerating a north wall.

'Dortmund' Large red flowers with a white centre. The flowers are single but carried in large clusters. Height 3.7 m (12 ft). This cultivar can also be grown as a shrub.

'Dublin Bay' Deep red flowers appearing throughout the summer, slightly scented. Height 2.5 m (8 ft).

'Étoile de Hollande, Climbing' Dark red flowers throughout the summer, sweetly scented. Height 3 m (10 ft).

'Grand Hotel' Bright red, double flowers shaded with scarlet, produced throughout the summer and having a faint elusive scent. Plentiful dark green, glossy leaves. Height 2.5 m (8 ft).

'Guinée' Scarlet flowers with a hint of black in the colour, scented. Height 3 m (10 ft).

'Parkdirektor Riggers' Brilliant crimson, semi-double flowers produced in large clusters throughout the summer. Height 3 m (10 ft).

'Paul's Scarlet Climber' Bright scarlet, semi-double flowers produced in large sprays in early summer. Height 4.5 m (15 ft). It is an old cultivar, and although it is sometimes recommended there are now many better kinds in the same colour range.

'Super Star, Climbing' Vermilion, with a pleasant perfume and long-lasting flowers produced throughout the summer. Height 2.5 m (8 ft). Its bold colour makes it attractive, but it is often an early victim of mildew and if it is grown the routine use of fungicidal sprays is recommended.

WHITE SHADES

'Elizabeth Harkness, Climbing' Creamy, fragrant double flowers produced throughout the summer. Height 3 m (10 ft).

'Iceberg, Climbing' Clear white, semi-double flowers in large clusters produced throughout the summer. Height 3 m (10 ft).

R. filipes 'Kiftsgate' Creamy white, small flowers, sweetly scented and produced in very large clusters in mid summer. The foliage is grey-green. Height 9 m (30 ft) or more. This plant is not one for walls, but will scramble over trees, through hedgerows or over sheds and buildings.

Rosa filipes 'Kiftsgate', a very vigorous rambler named after the fine Gloucestershire garden in which the original still grows

'Maigold' (see page 100)

R. longicuspis Creamy white, fragrant, single flowers, not unlike 'Kiftsgate' in its use and qualities. It does not grow quite as large, though it will reach 6 m (20 ft) in height.

'Wedding Day' Creamy white single flowers carried in very large clusters in mid summer. It is sweetly scented. Height 6 m (20 ft). It can be used to climb a tree or sprawl over a building, but it is not suitable for walls.

'White Cockade' White, scented double flowers produced throughout the summer. Dark green, healthy leaves. Height 2.1 m (7 ft).

YELLOW SHADES

'Breath of Life' Rich apricot-pink double flowers recurring throughout the summer. It can be grown as a distinctive shrub. Height 2 m (6 ft).

'Dreaming Spires' Bright yellow, sweetly scented flowers produced throughout the summer. Dark green leaves that contrast well with the flowers. Height 3 m (10 ft).

'Gloire de Dijon' Large, light yellow, sweetly scented double flowers produced throughout the summer. Height 3.5 m (11 ft). This is a very old cultivar; it has kept its place in catalogues principally because of its scent.

'Golden Showers' Bright yellow, scented, double flowers that become paler with age, recurring throughout the summer. Glossy, dark green leaves that set off the flowers. Height 3 m (10 ft). It is suitable for growing against a pillar or as a shrub.

'Highfield' Large, yellow, scented, double flowers. This is a sport of 'Compassion' (see page 97), and they make suitable neighbours on a wall or grown as shrubs. Height 3 m (10 ft).

'Maigold' Large, deep yellow, semi-double flowers blossoming most freely in early summer with fewer flowers later on. It has a strong scent. Height 3.5 m (11 ft). It can be grown as a shrub.

'Mermaid' Large, pale yellow single flowers with darker stamens, appearing intermittently throughout the summer and into early autumn. The glossy leaves contrast prettily with the flowers. Height up to 4.5 m (15 ft). This cultivar is sometimes difficult to establish, and rather slow-growing in its early years. It is, however, one of the classic roses and is worth persevering with if a south or west wall can be found for it. It can be badly cut back or even killed in a severe winter.

'Schoolgirl' Apricot double flowers, shaded with gold. These justify growing the plant, which gets bare and leggy at the base and might otherwise be rejected on this account. Height 3 m (10 ft).

'Sutter's Gold, Climbing' Yellow double flowers that appear early and recur through the summer. Height 3.5 m (11 ft). This cultivar possesses a strong scent, which justifies its continuing use after nearly 30 years.

CLIMBING SPORTS
There are many bush roses that have produced climbing forms known as sports. Some of the better ones are listed above, but there are several others still available from nurseries. They include the following: 'Caroline Testout' (pink), 'Cécile Brunner' (pink), 'Crimson Glory' (red), 'Ena Harkness' (red), 'Grandpa Dickson' (yellow), 'Lady Sylvia' (pink), 'Masquerade' (bicolour, yellow and red), 'Mrs Sam McGredy' (salmon).

They have been largely superseded as bush roses by improved selections, and the same fate is rapidly overtaking them in their manifestation as climbers. Potential purchasers should first look elsewhere.

Patio roses

Patio roses are Dwarf Cluster Flowered roses, separated in many catalogues from taller cultivars of the same type. The grouping has no official status, but it conveniently distinguishes the smallest cultivars. The name is already widespread and seems likely to establish itself. These roses have a distinct role in the garden: to edge paths or borders, for use in large containers or raised beds, and in flower-beds in small gardens where bigger roses would seem out of proportion.

PINK SHADES

'**Coral Reef**' Pink, semi-double with pretty buds.

'**Dainty Dinah**' Deep pink. The plants make an attractive, disease-resistant bush; it is one of the better darker pinks available.

'**Fairy Changeling**' Rose pink, which changes according to the age of the flower to produce an unexpected mixture of colours ranging through to magenta.

'**Gentle Touch**' Pale pink. The colour is particularly striking, and it is well worth growing where a pale shade is needed, perhaps to contrast with stronger colours like 'Drummer Boy'.

'**Little Jewel**' Rose pink.

'**Nozomi**' Pale pink to white. The trailing stems make it suitable for the top of a wall or for use in a container. It makes a very effective weeping standard. The flowers are single but are extremely attractive, and act as a foil to stronger colours.

'**The Fairy**' Rose pink. This cultivar flowers rather later than others but the foliage is attractive, particularly in spring.

'**Yesterday**' Lilac pink. This rose has an old-fashioned look that makes it attractive. It is strong enough to fit in a shrub border.

It is rather taller than most patio roses because of occasional taller shoots, which can be cut away if necessary or allowed to arch.

RED AND ORANGE SHADES

'**Anna Ford**' Orange-red, with many small, double flowers. Disease resistant.

'**Boys' Brigade**' Red, with a cream centre to the open, semi-double flower. Relatively tall. Disease resistant.

'**Buttons**' Salmon red. The buds are pretty and look attractive in a flower arrangement. The rose has been introduced very recently so it is not possible to say whether it is disease resistant, but like most others of this type it gives every evidence of good health.

'**Drummer Boy**' Crimson, with a splash of yellow at the centre of the flower when it is wide open. The colour is bright and cheerful.

'**Fairy Damsel**' Deep red.

'**Little Prince**' Orange red.

'**Marlena**' A bright crimson red. This is one of the taller cultivars. The edges of the petals are likely to blacken in hot, strong sun so it is better in cooler climates or in some shade. Disease resistant.

'**Robin Redbreast**' Dark red with a pale yellow, nearly white eye.

'**Stargazer**' Orange-red with a yellow eye.

'**Sweet Magic**' Orange with gold tints. The flowers are shapely and attractive in a flower arrangement, and like many patio roses make attractive small buttonhole flowers when in bud.

'**Wee Jock**' Deep crimson. Very attractive when in bud.

'Boys' Brigade'
(see page 101)

WHITE SHADES

'Hakuun' Buff to cream, with numerous flowers.

'Yvonne Rabier' White. This is an older cultivar that has remained in catalogues for nearly 80 years because of its pretty, miniature flowers. It has a pleasant fragrance and is generally disease resistant.

YELLOW SHADES

'Baby Bio' Bright yellow. The flowers do not fade as they get older, which is an advantage. Can grow to the taller end of the range. Disease resistant.

'Clarissa' Apricot with some pink in the flower. A taller cultivar, with rather upright growth.

'Kim' Yellow flushed with pink.

'Rugul' Bright yellow with small, attractive leaves.

'Peek-a-boo' Apricot with pink tones. A rather spreading plant, with numerous small flowers that are very pretty and of an unusual colour.

OTHER COLOURS

'International Herald Tribune' Violet with yellowish centres. The colour is very unusual. The bushes are small and compact for so large and spreading a name. Disease resistant.

'Regensberg' Pink petals with a white base and edge, with a conspicuous boss of stamens that make the flower both unusual and very pretty when open. This plant may need protection against black spot in some areas.

Miniature roses

Miniature roses are low-growing cultivars that are miniature not only in their height but also in the size of their leaves and flowers. In this respect they can be distinguished from patio roses, which usually have normal-sized leaves and blossoms.

Miniature roses have many devotees, and as the number of cultivars expand and their diversity increases they seem likely to become even more popular. They are best in window boxes, pots, troughs, containers and in rock gardens, where they extend the period of floral interest through the quieter seasons of summer and autumn. They are not robust enough to stand in the open garden, nor are they big enough to be displayed satisfactorily in flowerbeds, though this is sometimes recommended in gardening literature.

There are also miniature standards; cultivars like 'Baby Masquerade', 'Snowball', 'Snow Carpet' and 'Stacey Sue' are available in this form. They can be used wherever miniature roses themselves are suitable.

Not many are fragrant, but 'Angela Rippon', 'Sheri Anne' and 'Sweet Fairy' are scented, and several others, like 'Gold Pin' and 'Little Flirt', have a less noticeable perfume.

Most of the cultivars grow to between 30 cm (1 ft) and 45 cm (1 ft 6 in) in height, though cultural conditions have an important effect. For example, if they are dry or growing in poor soil they will be stunted; in rich soil, with ample moisture

'Snowball' (see page 105)

and warmth, they will grow to their maximum height.

Miniature roses require the same cultural techniques as other pot and container plants. They should be grown in a well-drained, fertile compost, given plenty of water during the growing season, and sprayed where necessary to keep pests and diseases at bay, though these are not likely to be very common. Aerosol sprays are useful.

If they are used as pot plants, they can be brought indoors for short periods of time, but should be kept cool and returned to the open air as soon as possible for fear of causing soft, weak growth. If several are grown it is possible to rotate them. When displayed in a house they should be kept on light windowsills because most rooms are too dark for them to grow satisfactorily. As house plants they make a good talking point, and visitors almost invariably notice them.

They need little or no pruning, but dead flowers should be removed and any dead shoots cut back to healthy, sound tissue.

Because they are normally sold in containers they can be planted at any time, but they establish with least trouble while they are dormant in late winter.

Miniature roses can be propagated on their own roots by means of half-ripe cuttings taken in mid summer. The cuttings should be about 7.5 cm (3 in) long and made from strong, healthy growth from the current year. Hormone rooting compounds are desirable to assist the speed of rooting; the cutting should be inserted about an inch deep in sandy compost in a cold frame or cool greenhouse. They can be propagated in a mistpropagation unit or in a propagation case, but because the plants are hardy they should not be left long in a warm place. Plants grown on their own roots are noticeably weaker in growth than those that are propagated by grafting or budding in a greenhouse. Most roses bought commercially will have been grafted; suckers may appear and should be removed as soon as possible.

All plants in containers require occasional new compost, which can be introduced by repotting every second year in the spring and by scraping away the top inch or so of the old compost and replacing it with new material in the alternate years. In larger containers or troughs they can grow for many years without being disturbed, but may need feeding if they show signs of weak growth or sickly, pallid leaves. Nutrients can be applied in a liquid form when watering, by foliar feeding to give a quick fillip, or by using ordinary rose fertilizer sprinkled sparingly on the surface of the soil just before growth starts and worked lightly in with a hand fork.

MULTICOLOURED SHADES

'Baby Masquerade' The double flowers vary in colour as they age, and range from yellow to pink and finally include red. Often all three appear together on the same flower.

'Little Artist' Red splashed with white. The flower is an attractive novelty and well worth considering.

'Little Flirt' Red with a yellow reverse, slightly scented. The flowers soon fade in prolonged sunshine or where light intensities are high.

'Magic Carrousel' Creamy white. The petals have a broad band of red at the edges. It is a very pretty plant in full flower.

'Toy Clown' White edged with carmine red. This cultivar does badly in places with colder winters, though its unusual flowers make it worth growing in warmer areas.

PINK SHADES

'Angela Rippon' Coral pink, scented and disease resistant.

'Dresden Doll' Shell pink with conspicuous golden stamens.

'Hollie Roffey' Rose pink. The flowers are pretty, with perhaps a superabundance of petals when fully open.

'New Penny' Pale coral pink.

'Royal Salute' Rose pink, slightly scented.

'Stacey Sue' Light pink, slightly scented.

'Sweet Fairy' Lilac pink. Known for its sweet scent.

'Teeny Weeny' Pink. The flowers are small and the name is of that syrupy kind that is endemic among miniature roses!

'Tiny Jill' Rose pink.

RED SHADES

'Darling Flame' Orange-red with a touch of yellow in the petals. A very bright, showy colour that stands out well in a container.

'Fire Princess' Orange-red, slightly scented. The bright colour shows up against the dark green foliage.

'Little Buckaroo' Deep red with a white centre. The generally healthy foliage is glossy and bronze.

'Orange Sunblaze' Bright orange red.

'Red Ace' Rich velvety red. The flowers make pretty cut flowers.

'Sheri Anne' Orange-red. Pretty flowers and foliage; possessed of a sweet perfume.

'Starina' Orange-red with a lighter, nearly golden reverse. It makes a pretty pot plant, and the flowers are attractive both as buds and when fully open.

'Wee Man' Scarlet, slightly scented.

WHITE SHADES

'Pour Toi' Creamy white. This is an older cultivar that has kept its place be-cause of its pleasant sympathetic colour and neat habit of growth.

'Snowball' White. This plant is very tiny, reaching little more than 15 cm (6 in) in height. It spreads, and plants can exceed 30 cm (1 ft) across. This gives a very unusual effect since it clads itself with white flowers.

'Snow Carpet' White. This plant spreads and can get as big as 60 cm (2 ft) across. Both this and 'Snowball' make attractive miniature standards.

YELLOW AND APRICOT SHADES

'Baby Sunrise' Pale orange and yellow.

'Gold Pin' Yellow, slightly scented.

'Rosina' Yellow. May need protection against black spot. This cultivar is also sold under the names 'Josephine Wheatcroft' and 'Yellow Sweetheart'. It is very pretty when in bud, but the open flower has a slightly ragged look.

'Yellow Doll' Light yellow, large, slightly scented flowers. Needs protection against black spot.

OTHER COLOURS

'Elfin' Pink with some mauve in the colour, therefore called bluish.

'Green Diamond' Whitish green. Worth considering as a novelty.

'Lavender Jewel' The colour is really pink with a touch of mauve.

'Mr Bluebird' Lavender with a trace of purple, certainly not blue, and only for those who wish to add to the colour range in their garden.

Shrub roses

Botanically speaking all roses are shrubs, and the use of the term 'shrub roses' is sometimes criticized when applied only to a particular group. It is, however, gaining common acceptance in catalogues and elsewhere, and it is used here as well. It has the advantage of implying the use of its cultivars as components of shrub borders, either with other plants or alone. In addition, some are valued as hedgerow plants and others are sold for use as ground cover, though few of them are ideal for the purpose. Also, few of them need regular pruning.

Plant breeders have been active, and although the group includes the old-fashioned roses there are new ones as well.

Some of the older kinds flower for a disappointingly short time. Their advocates point out that they have this in common with many other shrubs that are not criticized on this account, but there are now alternatives with long seasons of interest, and these can usually be chosen in place of those with only ephemeral beauty.

In the miscellany of cultivars that this group contains there are considerable differences in height and spread. This affects not only the plants' position in a shrub border but also the distance apart at which they are planted. The approximate dimensions are indicated for each, though in practice they vary in size depending on growing conditions.

Rosa gallica var. *officinalis*, the red rose of Lancaster

BICOLOURED SHADES

R. foetida 'Bicolor' (Austrian Copper Briar) Yellow outside, coppery red within. Stems occasionally produce flowers that are completely yellow. The flowers are single and appear in mid summer. They have a mildly unpleasant smell, but the plant has nevertheless survived in cultivation for centuries. It is prone to disease. Height 1.5 m (5 ft), spread 1.2 m (4 ft).

R. gallica 'Versicolor' Crimson, striped unevenly with white. The scented flowers appear in mid summer, and make a striking show during their season, which is all too short. Also known as 'Rosa Mundi', this cultivar is an ancient one and is still popular, though it is prone to mildew and needs routine protection. Can be used as a hedge. Height and spread about 1 m (3 ft).

'Camaieux' Rose pink, getting first darker and then paler with age, and striped with white. The sweetly scented flowers are very pretty, but appear for only a brief season in early summer. The bush usually needs protection against disease. It can be used as a hedge. Height 1 m (3 ft), and about the same in spread.

'Ferdinand Pichard' Red streaked with blush pink, or possibly pink streaked with

red! The flowers are scented, cup-shaped and pretty, and produced throughout the summer. The plant is disease resistant. Height 1.5 m (5 ft), spread 1.2 m (4 ft).

'Variegata di Bologna' White streaked with purple. The scented, cup-shaped flowers are fully double, and produced mainly in early summer but with some later ones as well. Prone to black spot. It will grow taller if supported against a pillar or wall. Height 2 m (6 ft), spread 1.5 m (5 ft).

PINK SHADES

R. centifolia 'Cristata' (Chapeau de Napoléon) Deep pink, scented, double flowers in mid summer. The cultivar is an old one but it holds its own because the sepals are deeply divided at the margins and this gives the buds the appearance of being enclosed in a tiny fern. Can be used in the middle of a border. Height 1.5 m (5 ft), spread 1.2 m (4 ft).

R. centifolia 'Muscosa' (common moss rose) Rose pink, scented, double flowers in mid summer. The stems and buds are covered in dense, moss-like aromatic glands, which give the plant its common name. Its best place is towards the front of a border where this rather subtle quality

'Camaieux'

Rosa glauca, also known as *R. rubrifolia*

can be appreciated. Height and spread 1.2 m (4 ft).

R. eglanteria (sweet briar) Pink single flowers in mid summer. This species does not justify a place in the garden in spite of its bright autumn hips and spicy leaves; its hybrids, such as 'Lady Penzance', 'Lord Penzance' and 'Meg Merrilies', share some of its characteristics and are to be preferred. Also known as *R. rubiginosa*. Height 3 m (9 ft), spread 2.5 m (8 ft).

R. elegantula 'Persetosa' (Farrer's threepenny-bit rose) Pink, scented, single flowers in mid summer. The flowers are very small and give the plant its common English name. The plant is pretty when in flower but not very showy. Its longer lasting merits are its dainty foliage and small red hips in the autumn. It can be used in the back of a border. Height 2 m (6 ft), spread 1.2 m (5 ft).

R. glauca Pink, single flowers in mid summer. Also known as *R. rubrifolia*. Grown for its pale purple leaves and its abundant red hips. For the middle or back of a border, or will make a good hedge. Height 2 m (6 ft), spread 1.5 m (5 ft).

R. moyesii f. **rosea** Pink, single flowers in early summer. Also known as *R. holodonta*. Grown for its fine, large orange-red hips, which are among the best ornamental fruits for the garden in autumn. Height 3 m (10 ft), spread 2 m (6 ft).

R. moyesii 'Sealing Wax' Bright pink, single flowers; fine red hips. Height 2.5 m (8 ft), spread 1.5 m (5 ft).

R. nitida Pink, scented, single flowers in mid summer, followed by small, round red hips. The leaves turn scarlet in autumn, though the colours are better in some years than others. Can be used at the front of a border or to make a low hedge. Height and spread 1 m (3 ft).

R. villosa (apple-bearing rose) Pink, scented, single flowers. Also known as *R. pomifera*. Worth growing only for its hips, which are large, round and orange-red. Height 2 m (6 ft), spread 1.5 m (5 ft).

R. virginiana Pink, scented, single flowers in summer. Round red hips and good red and yellow autumn colour. For the middle of a border or as a hedge. Height 1.5 m (5 ft), spread 1.2 m (4 ft).

'Ballerina' Pale pink with a white centre. Small single flowers in large clusters. Blooms throughout the summer. Good for use at the front of a border, as a specimen, or to form a low hedge. Height 1.2 m (4 ft), spread 1 m (3 ft).

'Bonica' Rose pink, double flowers throughout the summer. Bright though small hips in the autumn. This is a valuable plant for use as a hedge, at the front of a border or in a bed by itself. Disease resistant. Height 1.5 m (5 ft), spread 1.2 m (4 ft).

'Cécile Brunner' Light pink, double flowers throughout the summer. This cultivar is now over a century old, but remains popular because of the beauty of its tiny buds. It is suitable for the front of a border or as a specimen in a small garden. There is also a climbing form. Height 1.2 m (4 ft), spread 60 cm (2 ft).

'Céleste' Rose pink, sweetly scented, semi-double flowers in mid summer. Healthy grey-green leaves. The flowers are pretty, but their season comparatively short. Also known as 'Celestial'. Suitable for the back of a border or for a hedge. Height 2 m (6 ft), spread 1.2 m (4 ft).

'Complicata' Single, pink flowers with a paler centre. Mid summer. It is still sold but is hardly worth growing except in a large collection. Height 3 m (10 ft), spread 2 m (6 ft).

'Constance Spry' Rose pink, scented, double flowers in mid summer. Can be used as a climber. Not suitable for small gardens. Height and spread 2 m (6 ft).

'Cornelia' Pink, scented, semi-double flowers, carried in large clusters throughout the summer, but are often most numerous in the autumn. Suitable as a specimen or in the middle of a border. Height and spread 1.5 m (5 ft).

'Empress Josephine' Pink double flowers with darker veining in mid summer. This is an old cultivar that is still grown, but it is not recommended except for larger collections. Height and spread 1.2 m (4 ft).

'Fairyland' Pink, scented, double flowers throughout the summer. Spreading, so suitable for filling space or for the front of a border. Height 60 cm (2 ft), spread 1.2 m (4 ft).

'Felicia' Pale pink with a touch of yellow; scented, double flowers throughout the summer. Suitable for the front of a border, and makes an attractive specimen in a smaller garden. Height and spread 1.2 m (4 ft).

'Ferdy' Salmon pink, semi-double flowers making a spectacular show in early summer and then again in the autumn. Useful in the middle or front of a border, as a specimen or a hedge. Healthy, small, glossy leaves. Height and spread 1.5 m (5 ft).

'Fritz Nobis' Pale pink, scented, double flowers in mid summer. Disease resistant. The bush makes a fine show when in flower but is then rather dull throughout the summer, coming to life again in the autumn when it usually carries a heavy crop of small orange hips. It is a plant for the middle of the border, where it can be associated with other cultivars that can provide summer interest. Height 1.5 m (5 ft), spread 1.2 m (4 ft).

'Fru Dagmar Hastrup' Large, light pink, scented single flowers throughout the summer. The large, round, red hips are an added bonus. Suitable to fill an odd corner as a low hedge or at the front of a border. Height and spread 1 m (3 ft).

'Frühlingsmorgen' Pink with a yellow centre. Large, scented, single flowers produced mainly in early summer. Can be used towards the back of a border. Its upright growth makes it less suitable for specimen planting. Height 2 m (6 ft), spread 1.2 m (4 ft).

'Gertrude Jekyll' Rich pink, sweetly scented, double flowers in mid summer, with the possibility of a second crop later. Both the pretty colour and the scent make it well worth growing. It can be used in the middle of a border. Height and spread 1.5 m (5 ft).

'Grouse' Profuse pale pink, scented, single flowers in summer, with a sprawling habit. Disease resistant. Sold as ground cover, but the growth is insufficiently dense to suppress weeds. Can be used to sprawl down a bank or to fill a space where height is not required. Height 30 cm (1 ft), spread 3 m (10 ft).

'Hansa' Deep pink to purple, sweetly scented, double flowers throughout the summer. Large red hips. Disease resistant. Can be used in the front of a border or to fill a corner. Height and spread 1.2 m (4 ft).

'Heritage' Pale pink, scented, double flowers throughout the summer. The cup-shaped blooms are very pretty. Suitable for the front of a border. Height and spread 1.2 m (4 ft).

'Koenigin von Danemarck' Pink, sweetly scented, double flowers in mid summer. The scent is the reason it continues in cultivation. Height 1.2 m (4 ft), spread 1 m (3 ft).

'Lady Penzance' Pink with a yellow centre. Single flowers in mid summer that quickly pass, but the plant is esteemed for the strong scent of the leaves, which endures from spring to autumn. Cheerful red hips. Can be used as a hedge or in the back of a border, but it takes up a lot of space. Height 2.1 m (7 ft), spread 2 m (6 ft).

'Madame Isaac Pereire' Large, deep pink, double flowers. Sweetly scented, blooming throughout the summer. Justifies a place because of its strong scent. Can be used in the middle or back of a border, where other plants with stronger stems can give it support. Height 2.1 m (7 ft), spread 1.5 m (5 ft).

'Marguerite
Hilling'

'Madame Isaac
Pereire' (see page
109)

'Madame Pierre Oger' Pale pink, scented double flowers flushed with cream. Blooms recur after the first flush. The plant is grown because of the pretty cup-shaped flowers, but is so likely to get black spot that it is best avoided. Height and spread 1.2 m (4 ft).

'Maiden's Blush' Pale pink, scented, double flowers in mid summer. This is a very old cultivar that has survived in cultivation because of the prettiness of the flowers. Front or middle of the border. Can be used as a hedge. Height and spread 1.5 m (5 ft).

'Marguerite Hilling' Pale pink, scented, single flowers in early summer, with some flowers later. Can be used as a specimen, a hedge, or towards the back of a border, but it suffers badly from black spot and should not be chosen unless regular preventive spraying is possible. Height 2.1 m (7 ft), spread 2 m (6 ft).

'Mary Rose' Pink, scented, double flowers over a long season. Can be used at the front of a border. Height and spread 1.2 m (4 ft).

'Max Graf' Scented, pink, double flowers with a paler centre, flowering in mid summer on trailing stems. Can be used on banks or to fill space where height is not required. It is sold for ground cover, but to be effective in this role the ground must be kept free of perennial weeds until the canopy of growth is complete. Even then some attention is likely to be needed,

and may be awkward to give among the prickly stems. Height 60 cm (2 ft), spread 2 m (6 ft).

'Nymphenburg' Pink with some yellow at the centre. Scented, semi-double flowers throughout the summer. Can be used as a hedge, as a specimen, to grow with support to form a pillar, or in the middle or back of a border. Height 2 m (6 ft), spread 1.2 m (4 ft).

'Old Blush China' Pink, scented, semi-double flowers. This very old cultivar was one of those that helped to create the modern rose. Also known as 'Common Blush' or 'Blush China'. It can still be used effectively in the middle of a border because of its exceptionally long flowering season. Height 1.5 m (6 ft), spread 1.2 m (4 ft).

'Omar Khayyam' Clear pink, scented, double flowers. The rose is not really worth a place in a modern garden, but the story attached to it might make it of interest for reasons other than horticultural ones. It is claimed to have been propagated from a plant growing on the grave of Omar Khayyam, and brought into Britain to be put on the grave of his most famous translator, Edward Fitzgerald. Height 1 m (3 ft), spread 60 cm (2 ft).

'Penelope' Apricot pink, paling as the bloom ages. Scented and semi-double.

Can be used as a hedge in the middle of a border, or pruned and used in a flowerbed. Height 1.5 m (5 ft), spread 1.2 m (4 ft).

'Pheasant' Deep pink double flowers in summer. A vigorous spreading rose, well adapted for sprawling over a bank. Sold as ground cover. Height 30 cm (1 ft), spread 3 m (10 ft).

'Pink Bells' Pink double flowers throughout the summer. See also 'Red Bells' and 'White Bells' (pp. 113 and 115). Height 60 cm (2 ft), spread 1.2 m (4 ft).

'Pink Grootendorst' Bright pink, double flowers throughout the summer. The petal has a frilled edge not unlike some carnations. Suitable for the middle or front of a border. Height 1.2 m (4 ft), spread 1 m (3 ft).

'Pink Wave' Soft pink double flowers throughout the summer. Suitable for the front of a border or as a small specimen. Height 1.2 m (4 ft), spread 1 m (3 ft).

'Rosy Cushion' Rose pink, single flowers throughout the summer. Suitable for the front of a border. Height 1 m (3 ft), spread 1.5 m (5 ft).

'Souvenir de la Malmaison' Pale pink, double flowers throughout the summer. Sweetly scented. A plant for the middle or back of a border. This rose was seen at

'Max Graf'

'Moonlight' (see page 114)

Malmaison in the middle of the last century by the Grand Duke of Russia. He asked that it should be given a name that would honour the memory of the Empress Josephine, who had established the garden and the rose collection it still contains. Height and spread 2 m (6 ft).

'Stanwell Perpetual' Pale pink fading to white. Sweetly scented flowers throughout the summer, though never making the bold display of some other cultivars. Can be used in the middle of a border or as a hedge. The leaves often become spotted and discoloured; there is no remedy but the trouble does not spread. Height and spread 1.5 m (5 ft).

'The Fairy' Small, pink, double flowers throughout the summer. Spreading habit. Suitable for use at the front of a border or to form a flowerbed on its own. Height 60 cm (2 ft), spread 1 m (3 ft).

'Zéphirine Drouhin' Pink, sweetly scented, semi-double flowers throughout the summer. The stems are nearly always free from prickles. It can be used as a climber or, with support, to form a pillar. It will also make a rather sprawling shrub for the back of a border. It is very prone to disease, and will need routine protection in many areas. Height 2.5 m (8 ft), spread 2 m (6 ft).

RED AND ORANGE SHADES

R. gallica* var. *officinalis (apothecaries' rose) Red, scented, semi-double flowers in mid summer. Small but conspicuous hips. Prone to mildew. Height 1.2 m (4 ft), spread 1 m (3 ft).

Its physical attributes are not the real reason for growing this rose; if it relied on them alone it would have been entirely replaced by the better forms that are now available. Its long history allows it to keep its place. This ancient plant is believed to have been cultivated by the Romans. This is the rose that provided the emblem for the House of Lancaster in England's Wars of the Roses, and is also known as the rose of Provins.

R. moyesii Dark red, single flowers in mid summer. The flowers are small but conspicuous, and are followed by abundant, large, flask-shaped hips. The plant is chiefly grown for these. Height 3 m (10 ft), spread 2 m (6 ft). If allowed to grow without pruning the shrub becomes bare and leggy. Some of the oldest shoots should be cut down each year after the birds have harvested the fruit so as to ensure a supply of new young stems from the base.

***R. moyesii* 'Geranium'** Orange-red, single flowers in mid summer, followed by numerous red hips. It has the advantage over *R. moyesii* itself of a more compact habit, which makes it better for smaller gardens. Even so it needs plenty of space to look at home. Height 2.5 m (8 ft), spread 1.5 m (5 ft).

***R.* × *odorata* 'Mutabilis'** Scarlet buds, changing to sulphur yellow in the open flowers, which then darken to crimson. It produces its single flowers throughout the summer. Can be used as a climber or as a border plant. Height 2 m (6 ft) (but much taller when trained against a wall), spread 1.2 m (5 ft).

'Fiona' Red semi-double flowers throughout the summer. Sprawling habit; it is sold as ground cover, and can be used to fill a corner or in the front of a border. Height 1.2 m (4 ft), spread 2 m (6 ft).

'Highdownensis' Light red or deep pink, single flowers in mid summer. Long red hips adorn the arching branches in the autumn. Height 3 m (10 ft), spread 2 m (6 ft).

'Kassel' Scarlet double flowers throughout the summer. A plant for the middle of a border. Height 1.5 m (5 ft), spread 1.2 m (4 ft).

'Kordes Robusta' Scarlet single flowers throughout the summer. The large, bright green leaves show off the blossoms to advantage. Will make a dense thorny hedge. Height 1.5 m (5 ft), spread 1.2 m (4 ft).

'**Marjorie Fair**' Bright red with a white eye, with single flowers carried in large trusses that make a good show at the front of a border. Height 1.2 m (4 ft), spread 1 m (3 ft).

'**Meg Merrilies**' Crimson, scented, single flowers in mid summer. The leaves have a strong fragrance but are prone to disease. Attractive long hips in the autumn. It will make a good hedge with its very prickly stems, or a tall shrub for the back of a border. Height 2.5 m (8 ft), spread 2 m (6 ft).

'**Red Bells**' Bright red. Can be used as a front of border plant or as an edging or to trail over the side of a retaining wall. See also 'Pink Bells' and 'White Bells' (pp. 111 and 115). Height 60 cm (2 ft), spread 1.2 m (4 ft).

'**Red Blanket**' Rosy red, single flowers are shown to advantage against the dark, healthy leaves. Spreading habit. Can be used at the front of a border, or will make a rather wide hedge. Height 1 m (3 ft), spread 1.5 m (5 ft).

'**Red Max Graf**' Bright red, single flowers in clusters. Arching, spreading stems. Can be used at the front of a border, or as a ground filler when height is not required. Height 60 cm (2 ft), spread 1.5 m (5 ft).

'**Roger Lambelin**' Crimson with white edges to the petals, scented with double flowers throughout the summer. The flower is very pretty and unusual, but the plant may need protection from disease. Its place is the middle of a border. Height 1.5 m (5 ft), spread 1 m (3 ft).

'**Scarlet Fire**' Large, bright red, single flowers in mid summer. Bright red hips. Can be used as a specimen or in the back of a border. Height 3 m (10 ft), spread 2 m (6 ft).

'**William Shakespeare**' Deep red, sweetly scented double flowers over a long period. Height and spread 1.2 m (4 ft).

'**Zigeuner Knabe**' Crimson double flowers in mid summer. It is still widely grown, but it is a rather dull shrub that hardly justifies a place in the garden. Height and spread 1.2 m (4 ft).

WHITE SHADES

R. rugosa '**Alba**' White, scented, single flowers throughout the summer. Large, round red hips. A spreading, somewhat invasive shrub that excels as a ground filler or as a hedge. Bright green, wrinkled leaves and prickly stems that are typical of the species. Height and spread 1.5 m (5 ft).

R. sericea var. *omeiensis* forma *pteracantha* White, scented, flowering in early summer. This shrub is grown not for the flowers, which do not stay long enough to be of value, but for its prickles, which when young are crimson, and translucent when the sun shines against them. As they age they become grey and dowdy, but they present a formidable barrier when grown as a hedge. In a border the shrub should be pruned annually to encourage the growth of vigorous young stems on which the prickles are at their showiest. Height 2.5 cm (8 ft), spread 1.5 m (5 ft). The species is also known as *R. omeiensis* forma *pteracantha*.

'**Blanc Double de Coubert**' Pure white, sweetly scented, large flowers, double but not full. Blossoms throughout the summer. Leaves turn yellow in the autumn. The orange hips are large and showy but are not usually numerous. Disease resistant. Its thorny stems make a rather untidy barrier. Height 2 m (6 ft), spread 1.5 m (5 ft).

'**Blanche Moreau**' White, scented, double flowers appear in mid summer. This is one of the so-called moss roses, and this cultivar is interesting because of its dark-coloured 'moss'. Needs protection against disease and is not worth the space in a small garden. Height 1.2 m (4 ft), spread 1 m (3 ft).

'**Boule de Neige**' White with a little pink in the bud. Double, sweetly scented flowers. The main display is in mid summer, though they appear – albeit

‘Canary Bird’ (see page 116)

rather uncertainly – throughout the summer. May need protection against disease in some seasons. Height 1.5 m (5 ft), spread 1 m (3 ft).

‘Frau Karl Druschki’ White with a touch of pink in the bud. Double flowers throughout the summer. This cultivar is an old one and has several synonyms, including ‘White American Beauty’. Height 2 m (6 ft), spread 1 m (3 ft).

‘Frühlingsanfang’ Ivory white, single flowers in early summer. Not a plant for a small garden, but it makes a handsome specimen when planted alone or in a group of three with plenty of room for its arching stems to grow. Height 3 m (10 ft), spread 2 m (6 ft).

‘Madame Hardy’ Creamy white, becoming pure white with age. Double, sweetly scented flowers in mid summer. Height and spread 1.5 m (5 ft).

‘Moonlight’ Creamy white, scented, semi-double flowers that appear throughout the summer, often in very large clusters. Can be grown as a rather sprawling shrub, or encouraged to clamber through the branches of a small tree. Height 2.1 m (7 ft), spread 1.2 m (4 ft).

Rosa chinensis ‘Viridiflora’, the green rose (see page 116)

‘Nevada’ Creamy white, but pink in the bud; semi-double flowers in early summer with occasional flowers later. Prone to black spot; its vigour allows it to shrug off the infection, but if other roses are nearby the disease should be controlled to prevent it from spreading. In full flower the plant is gorgeous. It can be used in a shrub border placed towards the back, as a specimen or to form a hedge, but the stems have few prickles and this can be a disadvantage on a boundary. Height and spread 2 m (6 ft).

‘Partridge’ White, scented, single flowers in summer. This is a vigorous prostrate shrub often sold for ground cover, but its growth is not sufficiently dense to suppress all weeds so it is not truly effective in this role unless weedkillers are also used. The ground should also be free of perennial weeds before planting. Height 30 cm (1 ft), spread 3 m (10 ft).

‘Paulii’ White, scented, single flowers in mid summer. It is spreading and prickly; used as a ground filler but otherwise not worth growing. Height 1 m (3 ft), spread 3 m (10 ft).

‘Pearl Drift’ White with a blush of pink, with nearly double flowers. It makes a pretty specimen, or it can be used at the front of a shrub border. Height and spread 1 m (3 ft).

'Prosperity' Creamy white, flushed with pink. It has sweetly scented, double flowers throughout the summer. Height 1.5 m (5 ft), spread 1.2 m (4 ft).

'Sally Holmes' Ivory white, scented, single flowers throughout the summer. This cultivar makes a showy plant for the front of a border, or can be used as a low hedge or even in a bed by itself. Height 1.2 m (4 ft), spread 1 m (3 ft).

'Schneezwerg' White, slightly scented, semi-double flowers throughout the summer. Bright red, though rather small hips that start to appear early and make a pretty contrast with the later flowers. Suitable for use as a hedge or in the middle of a border. Height and spread 1.5 m (5 ft).

'Swany' White, double flowers throughout the summer. The leaves are small and shiny, and together with the small flowers have a fine texture that allows the plant to find a place as an edging for beds or borders of other cultivars. It can also be used to trail over the edge of a container. Height 60 cm (2 ft), spread 1 m (3 ft).

'White Bells' White double flowers that are small but numerous and appear throughout the summer. Arching, sprawling habit of growth. It has the same range of uses as 'Swany'. It can be used with 'Pink Bells' and 'Red Bells' (see pages 111 and 113) to make a splash of colour. Height 60 cm (2 ft), spread 1.2 m (4 ft).

YELLOW AND APRICOT SHADES

R. primula Pale yellow, single flowers in late spring. The flowers are scented, but it is worth growing principally for its aromatic foliage. Height and spread 1.5 m (5 ft).

'Charles de Mills'
(see page 117)

'Agnes' Apricot at the centre of the flower, fading to cream. Sweetly scented, fully double flowers. The main season of blossom is in early summer, but it flowers erratically thereafter. This is a hybrid of *R. rugosa* × *R. foetida*, and the thorny stems it has inherited make it a good plant for a barrier. Height 2 m (6 ft), spread 1.5 m (5 ft).

'Anna Zinkeisen' Yellow at the centre, paling to ivory. Scented, double flowers that open wide enough to show the stamens at their heart. Height 1.2 m (4 ft), spread 1 m (3 ft).

'Buff Beauty' Apricot fading to pale yellow. Sweetly scented, double flowers intermittently throughout the summer. Can be used as a hedge or in a border. Height and spread 1.5 m (5 ft).

'Cantabrigiensis' Pale yellow single flowers in late spring and early summer. It is among the first roses to appear. Dainty leaves, which in some seasons have a pretty though not flamboyant autumn colour. Small, orange-red hips. This rose was bred at the University of Cambridge Botanic Garden, hence its name. Height 2.1 m (7 ft), spread 2 m (6 ft).

'Canary Bird' Deep yellow, scented single flowers in late spring and early summer. When the plant is doing well it makes a fine sight, with its numerous flowers and dainty leaves carried on graceful arching stems. It will form a strong, attractive hedge or specimen plant. Height 2.5 m (8 ft), spread 2 m (6 ft).

'Chinatown' Yellow edged with pink, its scented double flowers appearing throughout the summer. Disease resistant. Makes a good hedge or an attractive specimen plant. Height 1.5 m (5 ft), spread 1 m (3 ft).

'English Garden' Yellow, darker towards the centre, with slightly scented, double flowers throughout the summer. This plant can be used at the front of a border, where it makes a cheerful splash of colour. Height 1 m (3 ft), spread a little less.

'Frühlingsgold' Rich yellow, fading as the flowers get older. The large, semi-double flowers open wide to display conspicuous stamens. The scent is strong and pervasive. The main display occurs in early summer, but some flowers do appear later on as well. This is a shrub for larger spaces only, but if there is room it makes a fine specimen when planted on a lawn, where its arching graceful stems can be seen to their best effect. Height 2.1 m (7 ft), spread 2 m (6 ft).

'Golden Wings' Yellow, the colour deepening towards the centre. Single, scented flowers throughout the summer. A fine showy plant for the middle or back of a border. Height 2 m (6 ft), spread 1.5 m (5 ft).

'Graham Thomas' Deep yellow, scented, with double, cup-shaped flowers throughout the summer. Height and width 1.2 m (4 ft).

'Helen Knight' Bright yellow, single flowers in late spring and early summer. The dainty leaves and dark stems enhance a pretty background. Height 2 m (6 ft), spread 1.5 m (5 ft).

'Lord Penzance' Yellow tinged with pink towards the edges of the petals, flowering in mid summer. The foliage of this cultivar is scented, like others derived from the sweet briar. It is at its best when the leaves are wet after rain. Black spot can be troublesome. Height 2 m (6 ft), spread 1.5 m (5 ft).

'Thisbe' Pale yellow, darker in the bud. It is musk scented, this being its principal merit. Flowers are produced throughout the summer. Height and spread 1 m (3 ft).

OTHER SHADES

***R. chinensis* 'Viridiflora'** Green blotched with purple; double flowers throughout the summer. The flowers are not pretty but they are curiosities, and may be attractive to gardeners who wish to confuse their neighbours or who prefer novelty to beauty in flower arrangements. Even then one plant should be enough! Its place is the front of a border. Height and spread 1 m (3 ft).

R. rugosa The reddish purple and sweetly scented single flowers occur throughout the summer. The large, orange-red hips are very fine. Can be used to make a boundary hedge, as a ground filler or planted towards the back of a border. Height 2.1 m (7 ft), spread 2 m (6 ft).

'Belle de Crécy' Dark pink, turning to purple and then to mauve as the flowers age. The scented flowers are double. Makes a rather untidy bush. Height 1.5 m (5 ft), spread 1 m (3 ft).

'Cardinal de Richelieu' Purple, scented, double flowers in mid summer. Not a very cheerful colour for a garden except when the sun strikes it, but still grown after nearly a century and a half. It needs brighter neighbours to cheer it up. May need protection against disease. Height 1.2 m (4 ft), spread 1 m (3 ft).

'Cardinal Hume' The purple, scented, double flowers of this more up-to-date cardinal offer a more protracted season of interest, though the colour is much the same in the newly opened flower. Height 1 m (3 ft), spread 1.2 m (4 ft).

'Charles de Mills' Purple, scented, double flowers in mid summer; they are large and complex. Height and spread 1.2 m (4 ft).

'Lavender Lassie' Lilac pink, sweetly scented, double flowers throughout the summer in large clusters. An attractive, reliable plant for the middle of a border. Height 1.5 m (5 ft), spread 1.2 m (4 ft).

'Roseraie de l'Haÿ' Purple, sweetly scented, semi-double flowers throughout the summer. It shows its relationship with R. rugosa in its thick, wrinkled, dark green leaves, which turn yellow in the autumn. Can be used as a boundary hedge or towards the back of a border. Height 2.1 m (7 ft), spread 2 m (6 ft).

'Scabrosa' Large, mauve-red, sweetly scented, single flowers, followed by round red hips. The potential uses are the same as for other hybrids of R. rugosa (see above). Height 2.1 m (7 ft), spread 2 m (6 ft).

'William Lobb' Purple fading to lavender; scented, double flowers in mid summer. The buds are covered in dense green bristles, but they are not enough to rescue the gloomy colour that emerges once they open. Height 2.1 m (7 ft), spread 1.5 m (5 ft).

Glossary

anther The pollen-bearing part of the male organs or stamens of a flower, often an attractive feature in roses with single or semi-double flowers.

aphis The scientific name for aphids, a common insect pest of roses. There are many kinds, but all obtain their food by sucking the juices of the plant.

bicolor Having two distinct colours.

bonemeal A manure derived from animal bones, which are crushed to varying degrees of fineness. The larger the particles the slower the release of the nutrients. The finest grade, known as bone flour, is quick acting. All forms supply phosphates and smaller amounts of nitrogen. It is now sold in a sterilized form because of the risk of anthrax.

bud a rudimentary branch of a flower.

budding A form of grafting in which the bud of a chosen plant is inserted into the lower stem of another plant, which is used to provide the root system and in the case of standard roses the stem as well.

clone A group of individuals derived originally from a single plant and maintained by vegetative propagation.

Cluster Flowered Part of the classification of hybrid roses introduced by the International Federation of Rose Societies, in this case displacing the term Floribunda. The flowers may be single, semi-double or double, but the main feature of the group is that the flowers are produced in multi-stemmed trusses or clusters composed of many stems.

cultivar A garden variety, or form found in the wild, which is maintained as a clone in cultivation, e.g. 'Agnes'.

fertilization The union of male and female cells in the ovary of a flower.

forma A subdivision of a variety, used to mark botanically minor variations.

fungicide A chemical used to kill fungi, which on roses cause diseases such as black spot, rust and mildew.

genus A group of species with important characteristics in common, e.g. *Rosa*.

heeling in Temporary planting pending permanent placement.

hybrid A plant produced by crossing two distinct species, subspecies, varieties or cultivars with one another.

hybridization The crossing of two plants in order to create a new plant.

insecticide Any substance that will kill insects, and popularly by extension mites and other pests as well. Substances used primarily against mites are sometimes known as acaricides.

Large Flowered A term introduced as part of the reclassification of hybrid roses. (See also the term Cluster Flowered.) The distinguishing feature of the group is that the plants within it should all have shapely buds opening into large or medium-sized flowers, each placed individually on a long stalk.

mulch A dressing, usually of organic matter, applied to the surface of the soil with a view to suppressing the growth of weeds. It is popularly supposed by gardeners to assist in water retention by the soil, but this has not been demonstrated scientifically.

organic matter Materials that are derived, more or less directly, from plants and animals, e.g. bonemeal, seaweed, dried blood.

Opposite: That remarkable rambler *Rosa filipes* 'Kiftsgate' in its element, wreathing a tree in tiny single white blooms in the gardens of Chatsworth, Derbyshire

pergola A series of arches, usually crossing a walk.

petal In roses, the brightly coloured part of the corolla, which is the collective name for the petals and sepals together.

pollination The transfer of pollen from the anthers to the stigma of either the same or another flower.

propagation Any method employed to increase plants, e.g. seed cuttings, grafting.

raffia A plant fibre obtained from a species of palm. It was once a common binding material, but it has almost been superseded by modern alternatives.

scale insects Insects that during part of their life cycle attach themselves like minute limpets to the stems or leaves of plants and feed on the sap.

scion A term used in grafting for the bud or shoot separated from its parent and joined to the lower part of another plant or stock, which provides the root system.

sepal In roses, one of the five parts of the green calyx outside the coloured petals.

soft growth Stems that have not been hardened or matured by exposure to cool or dry conditions, and that are likely to be killed by frost.

species Basic unit of classification. A species is composed of similar but distinct individuals that interbreed freely among themselves, e.g. *Rosa moschata*, the musk rose.

spit In horticulture one spade's depth, normally about 30 cm (1 ft).

sport A mutation resulting from genetic changes in the apical meristem or growing point of a stem. It can cause variation in habit of growth, for example by producing extra long stems, as in the case of some climbing roses, or a change in flower colour.

stigma The tip of the style, which receives the pollen. It becomes sticky when the ovules are ready to be fertilized.

stock A plant used to furnish the root system in budding or grafting.

stratification Exposing seed to cold temperatures by placing them between layers (strata) of sand or other material.

sucker Growths arising from the stock of plants that have been budded or grafted; it also signifies any shoot growing separately from the root system.

trellis A frame or lattice of wooden bars crossing either at right angles or diagonally, and used to support climbing plants.

variety A unit of classification below species or subspecies, composed of individuals differing from the species in comparatively minor characteristics, e.g. *R. gallica* var. *officinalis*.

vegetative propagation A method of reproducing plants other than by seed, e.g. cuttings, layers.

vernalization The process of producing chemical changes within a seed (normally by winter cold), which permits its germination and without which the seed remains dormant and will not grow.

Bibliography

There is a considerable amount of literature on roses which reflects the centuries old prominence of the plant. The following are some of the books that are currently available from publishers.

Beales, Christopher *Classic Roses*. Collins Harvel, 1985.

Charlton, Don *Roses. Growing and Showing*. David and Charles 1984.

Gault, S. Millar and Synge, Patrick *Dictionary of Roses in Colour*. Mermaid Books, 1985.

Gibson, Michael *Growing Roses*. Croom Helm, 1985.

Griffiths, Trevor *Book of Classic Old Roses*. Michael Joseph, 1987.

Harkness, Jack *The Makers of Heavenly Roses*. Souvenir Press, 1985.

Harkness, Peter *Modern Roses*. Century Publishing Co., 1987.

Jekyll, Gertrude and Mawley, Edward *Roses for English Gardens*. George Newnes, 1902; Antique Collector's Club, 1982.

Krussmann, Gerd *Roses*. Timber Press, Portland, Oregon 1981; Batsford, London 1982.

Spuy, Kenneth R. van der *How to Grow Roses in the Southern Hemisphere*. Juta, 1976.

Thomas, Graham Stuart *Climbing Roses Old and New*. Dent, 1983.

Thomas, Graham Stuart *Shrub Roses of Today*. Dent, 1980.

Thomas, Graham Stuart *Old Shrub Roses*. Dent, 1979.

Curtis's *Botanical Magazine* (now *The Kew Magazine*). This publication still maintains its long tradition of fine colour printing and articles on plants, plant collecting and conservation. Since it was established in 1787 nearly 10,500 colour plates have appeared by many of the best British botanical artists.

Many national rose societies have regular publications and newsletters and arrange shows and lectures. They are worth joining for this and for the contact they bring with other growers and gardeners with a mutual interest in roses. The following is the list of members of the world federation of rose societies.

Argentina
Asociacion Argentina de Rosicultura
Peru 360, 5° piso, Dep. 20, 1068 Buenos Aires

Australia
The National Rose Society of Australia
271b Belmore Road, North Balwyn, Victoria 3104

Belgium
Societe Royale Nationale *Les Amis de la Rose*
Mullemstraat 14, B 9762 Mullem (Oudenaarde)

Bermuda
The Bermuda Rose Society
P.O. Box PG 162, Paget 6

Canada
The Canadian Rose Society
20 Portico Drive, Scarborough, Ontario M1G 3R3

China
Beijing Rose Society China
A2 Wanshousi Haidian, Beijing

France
Societe Francaise des Roses
Parc de la Tete d'Or, 69459 Lyon, Cedex 3

Germany
Verein Deutscher Rosenfreunde E.V.
Waldseestrasse 14, 7570 Baden Baden

Great Britain
The Royal National Rose Society
Chiswell Green Lane, St Albans, Hertfordshire AL2 3NR

Holland
Nederlandse Rozenvereniging
Kievitweg 5, 5752 PT Deurne

India
The Indian Rose Federation
438 Pushpam – 10th Road, Chembur, Bombay, 400-071

Israel
The Israel Rose Society
The Wohl Rose Park of Jerusalem, Kiryat Ben-Gurion, P.O. B. 1312, Jerusalem 91012

Italy
Associazione Italiana della Rosa
c/o Mrs Elena Fumagalli, Villa Reale, 20052 Monza

Japan
The Japan Rose Society
4-12-6 Todoroki, Setagaya-Ku, Tokyo 158

Luxembourg
Letzeburger Rousenfrenn
51 Ave du 10 Septembre, Luxembourg

New Zealand
The National Rose Society of New Zealand
P.O. Box 66, 17 Erin Street, Bunnythorpe, Palmerston North

Northern Ireland
Rose Society of Northern Ireland
13 Glen Ebor Park, Belfast BT4 2JJ

Norway
Norwegian Rose Society
Postboks 9008 Vaterland, 0134 Oslo 1

Poland
The Polish Society of Rose Fanciers
c/o Mrs Irena Gotzbiowska, Warszawa B 6, Browiewskigo 19 M7

South Africa
The Federation of Rose Societies of South Africa
c/o Mrs P. Kolbe, 5 Douglas Street, Waverley, Johannesburg 2090

Switzerland
Gesellschaft Schweizerischer Rosenfreunde
c/o Ingenieurschule ISW, Gruntal, CH-8820 Wadenswil

USA
The American Rose Society
P.O. Box 30.000, Shreveport, LA 71130

Uruguay
Asociacion Uruguaya de la Rosa
c/o Mrs Mercedes Drever de Villar, L. Cavia 3099 Apt 11, Montevideo

Zimbabwe
The Rose Society of Zimbabwe
c/o John R. B. Dunlop, P.O. Box HG 366, Highlands, Harare

Acknowledgements

Line artwork by Vana Haggerty

Photographs
Pat Brindley, pages 18, 34; Crown copyright © reproduced with the permission of the
Controller, Her Majesty's Stationery Office, and the Director, Royal Botanic Gardens, Kew,
pages 6, 10, 14; The Hamlyn Publishing Group Limited/W. F. Davidson, pages 38, 94
(bottom); The Hamlyn Publishing Group Limited/Andrew Lawson, page 74; Andrew
Lawson, pages 66, 99 (top), 110 (bottom), 118; Anthony Martin, pages 43, 58, 90 (top and
bottom), 91 (top and bottom), 95, 98 (bottom), 102, 111 (bottom), 114 (top); Victoria
Matthews, page 30, 39, 79, 99 (bottom), 106, 107 (top), 114 (bottom), 115; Octopus Books
Limited/George Wright, page 46; Photos Horticultural, pages 78, 83, 110 (top), 111 (top);
The Harry Smith Horticultural Photographic Collection, pages 23, 26, 27, 47, 50, 51, 54, 62,
71, 86–7, 98 (top), 103, 107 (bottom); David Welch, pages 22, 94 (top).

The Publishers and Anthony Martin would like to thank Colonel Ken Grapes, Secretary,
The Royal National Rose Society and David Castleton, Parks Superintendent, Regent's
Park, for permission to photograph at The Royal National Rose Society's Gardens, St
Albans and Queen Mary's Garden, Regents Park.

Taxonomy checked by Susyn Andrews, who works as a botanist at the Royal Botanic
Gardens, Kew, and is also a member of the *Kew Magazine* Editorial Committee. She studied
amenity horticulture at the National Botanic Gardens, Glasnevin, Co. Dublin, Republic of
Ireland.

Index